SAINTS

COLORING BOOK

This book belongs to:

____

____

____

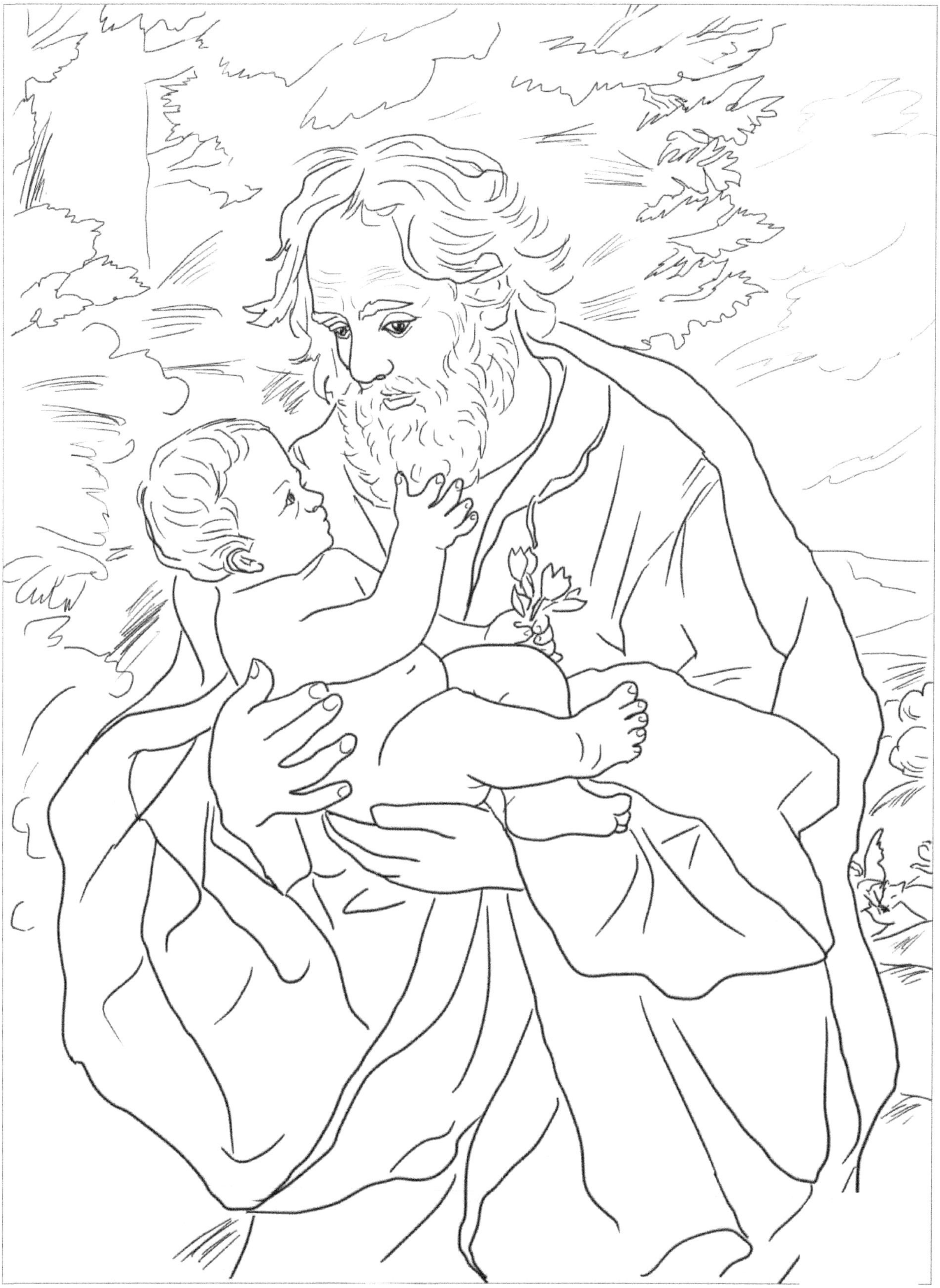

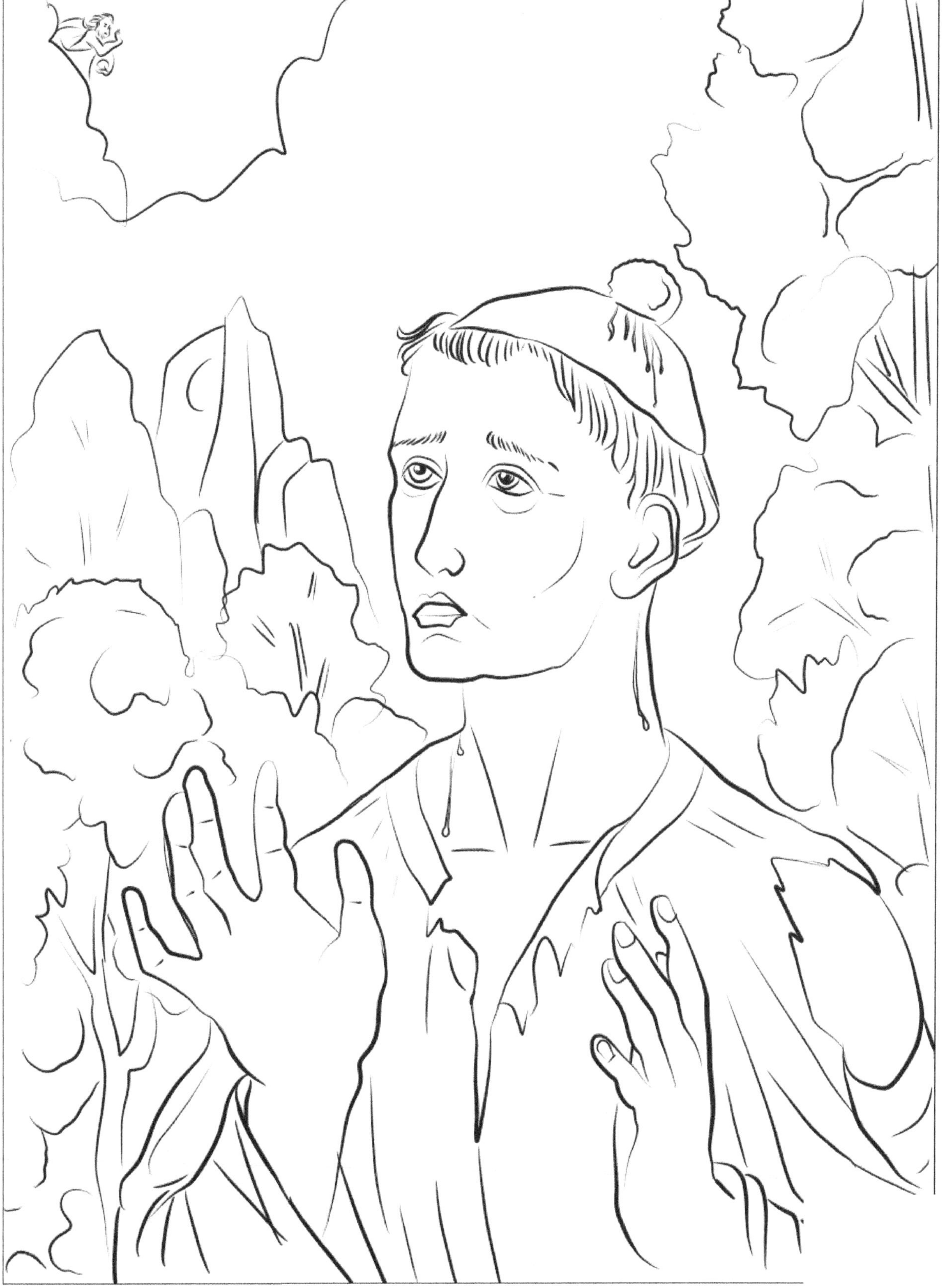

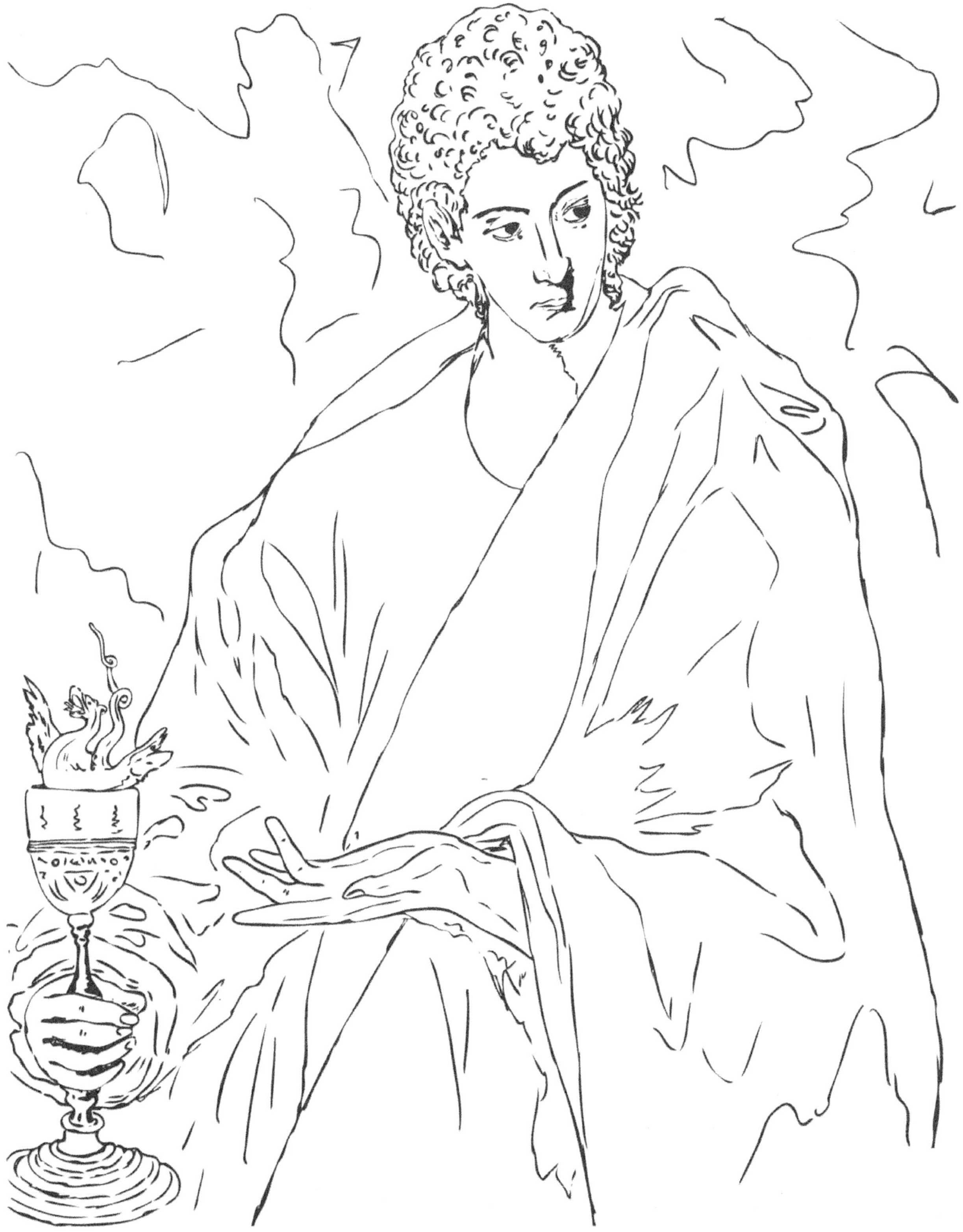

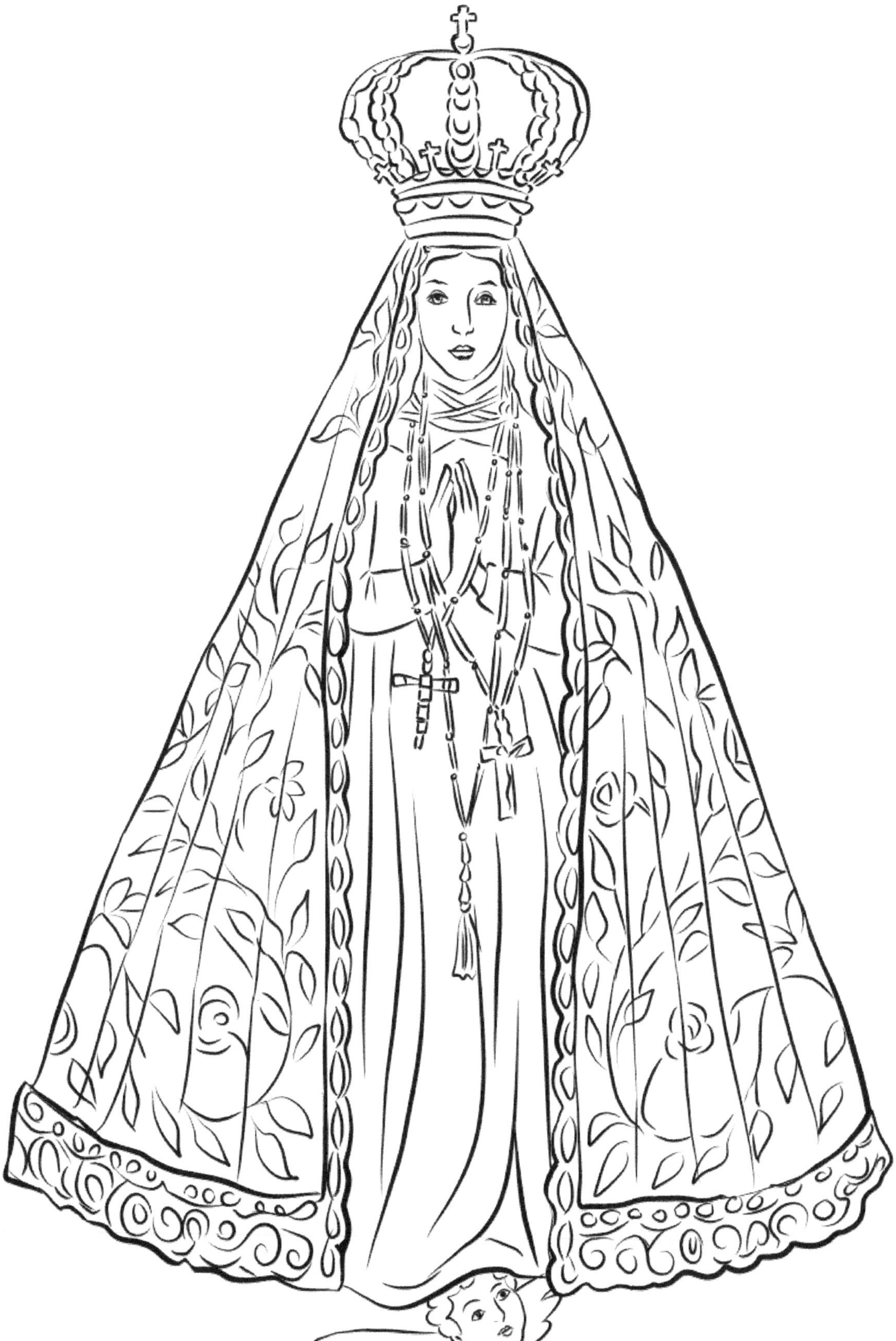

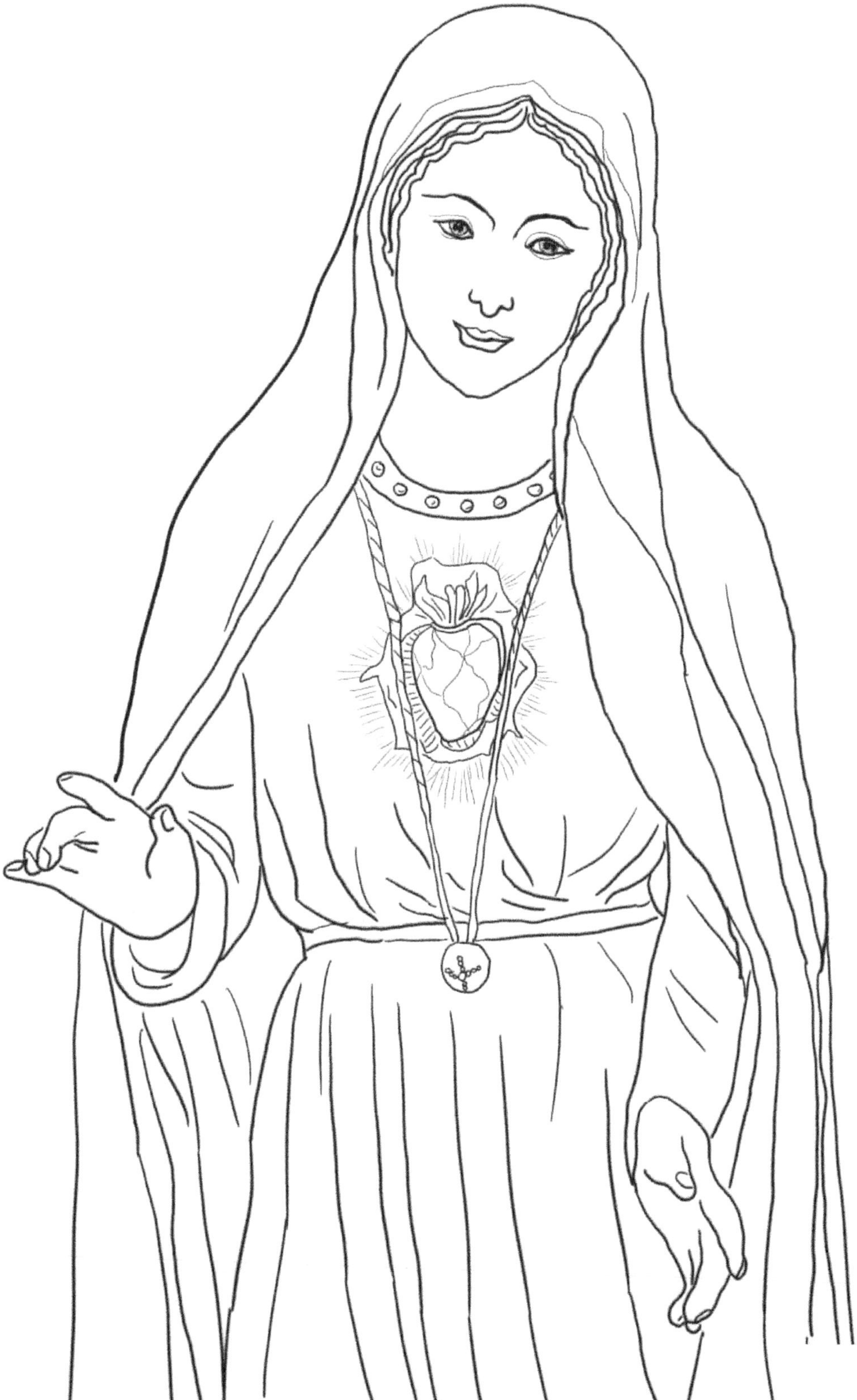

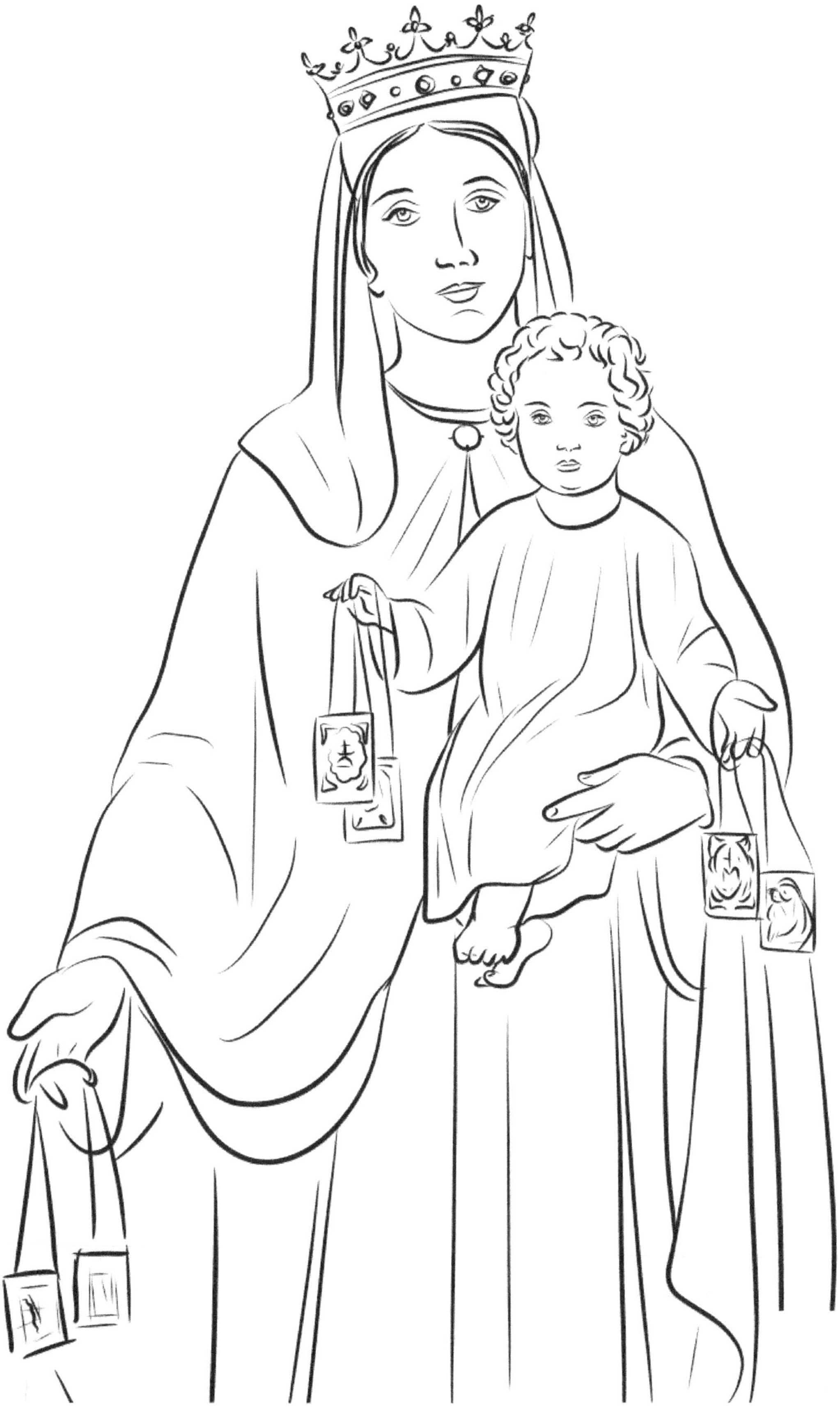

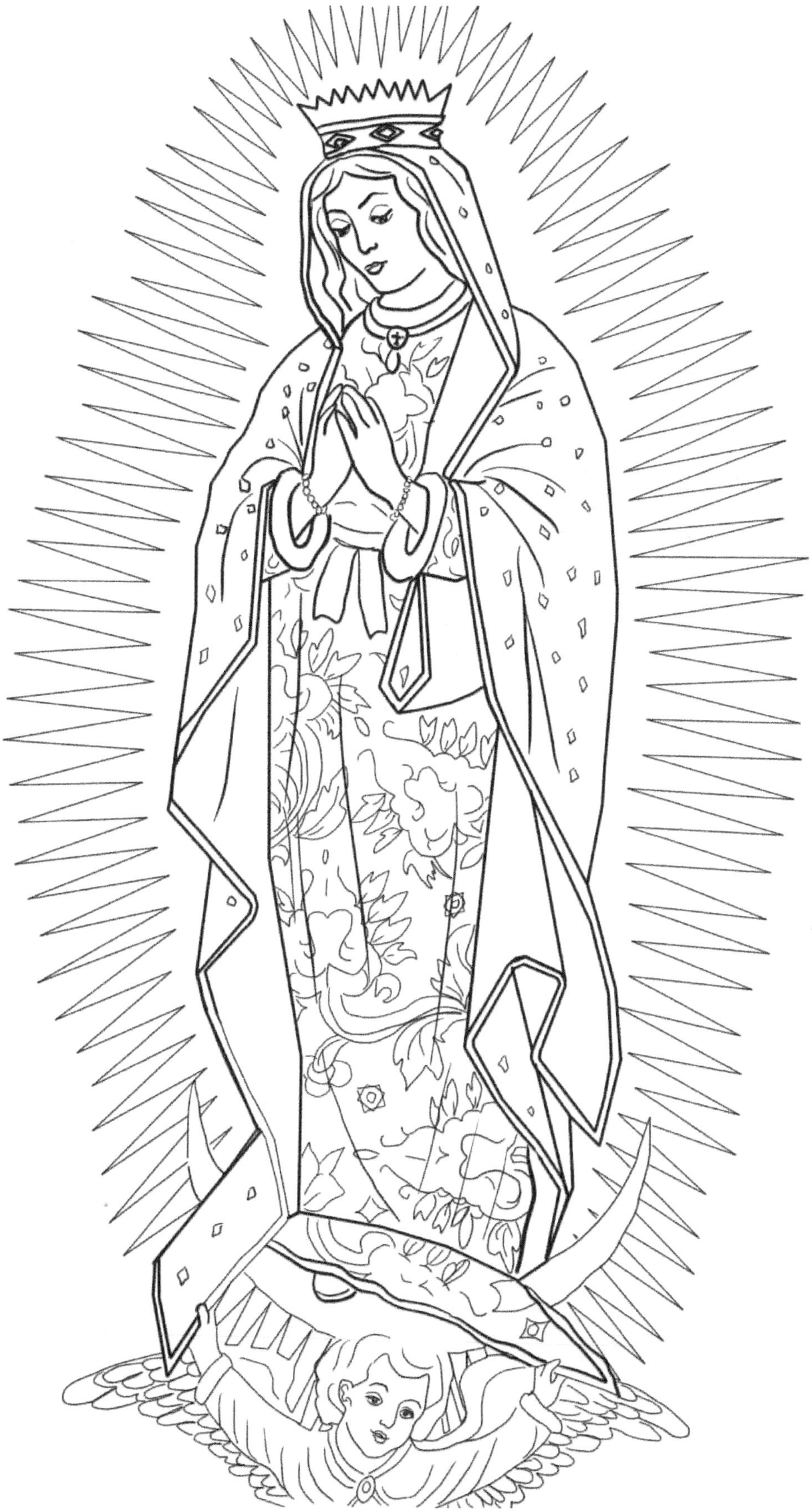

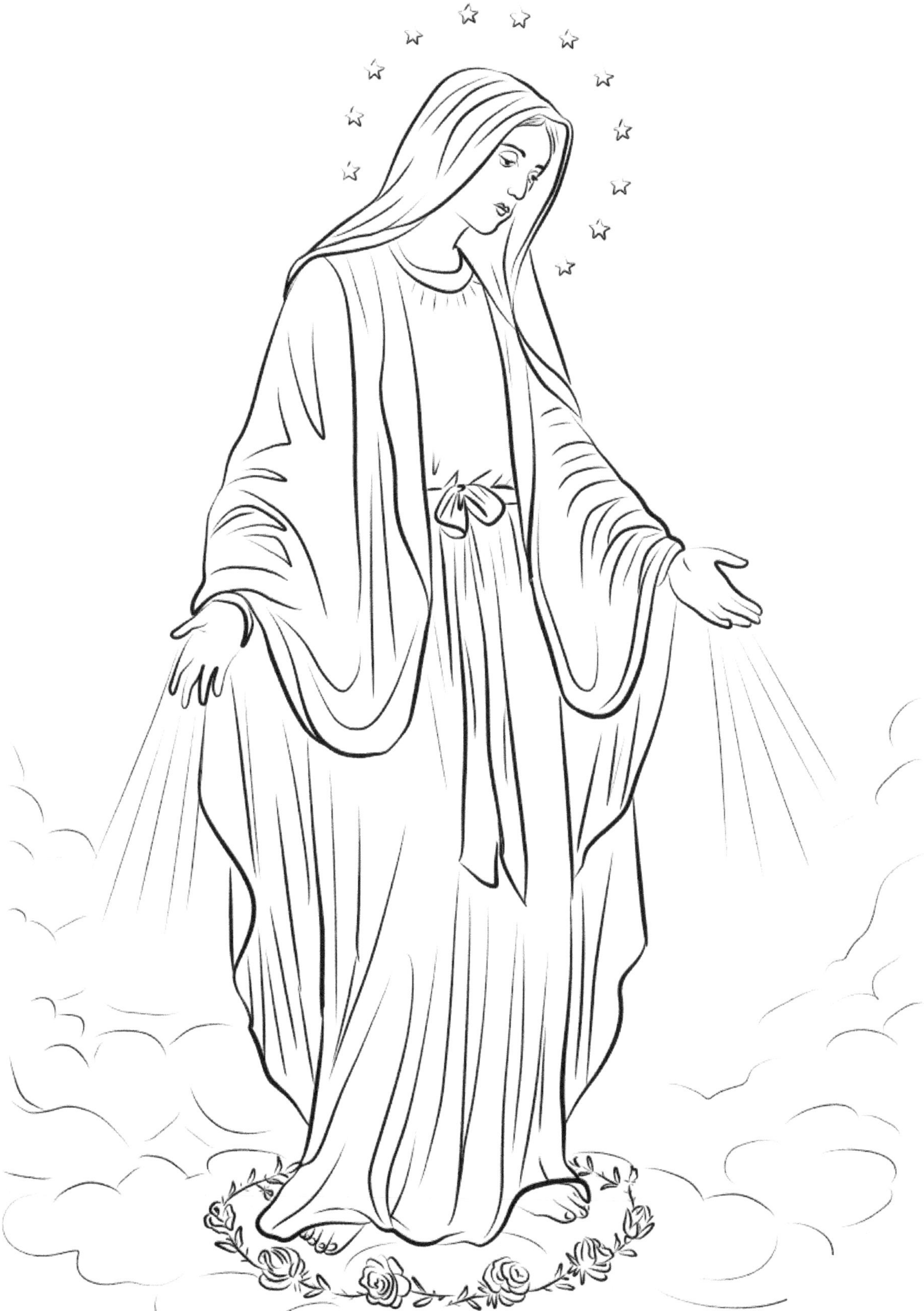

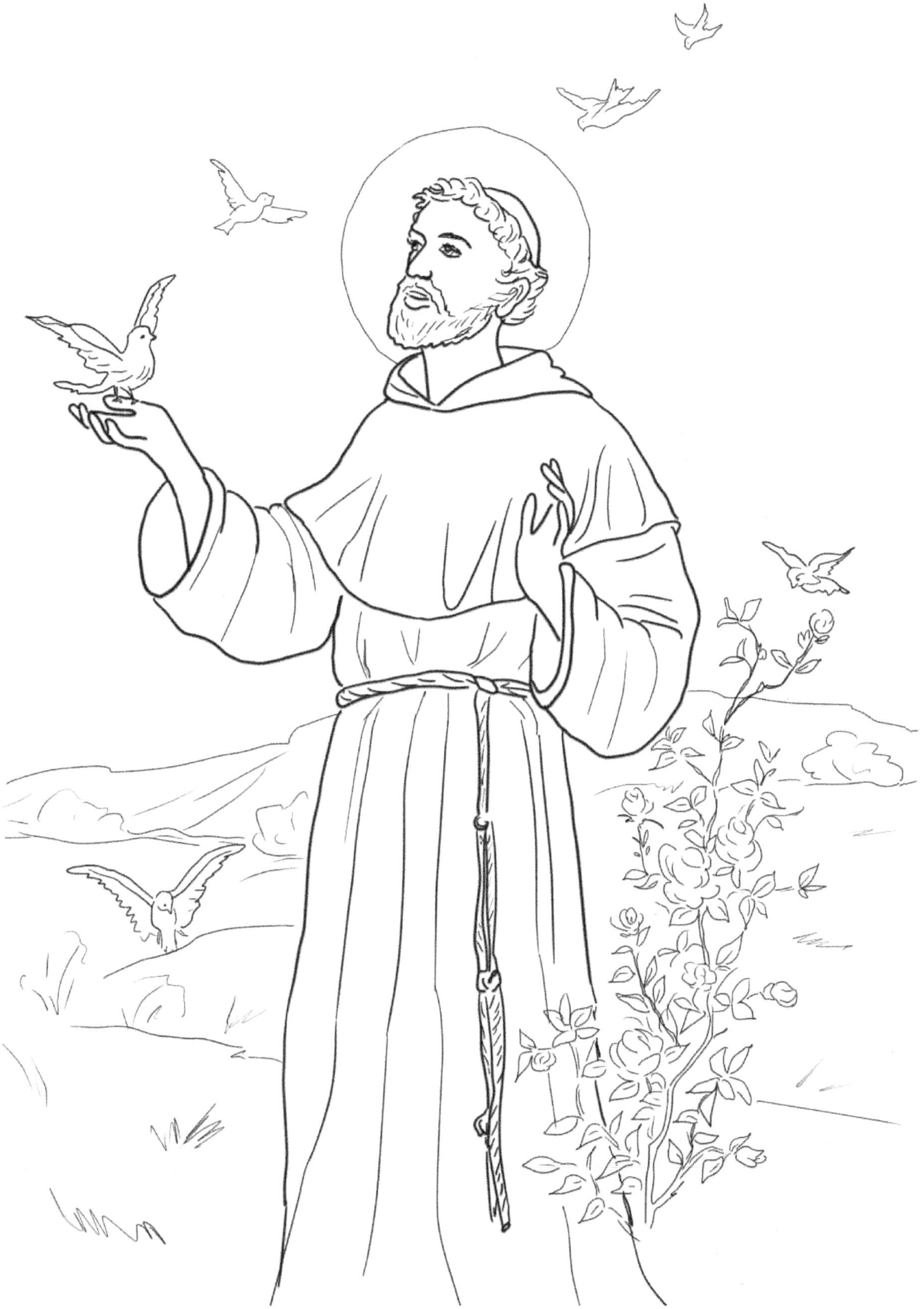

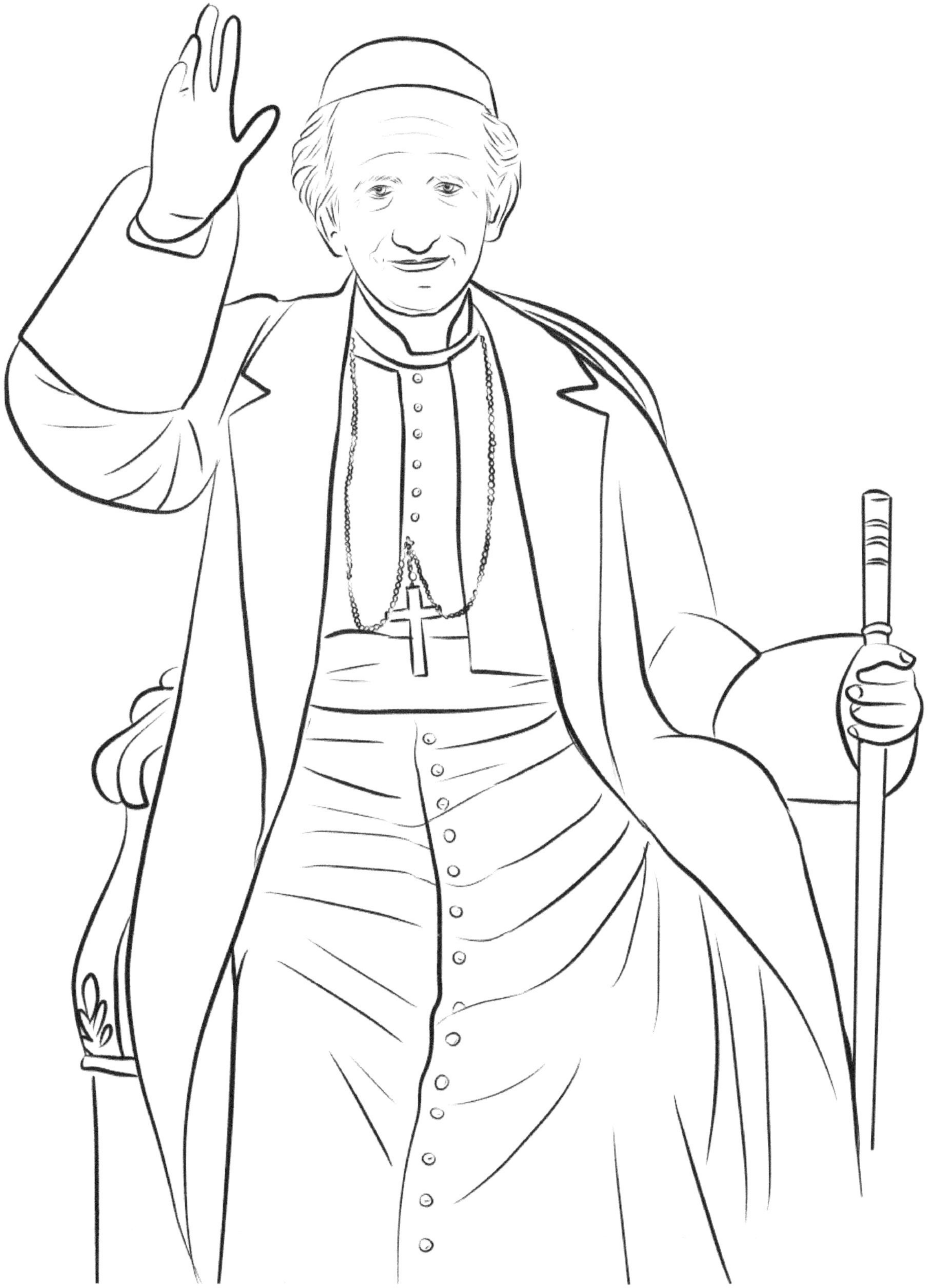

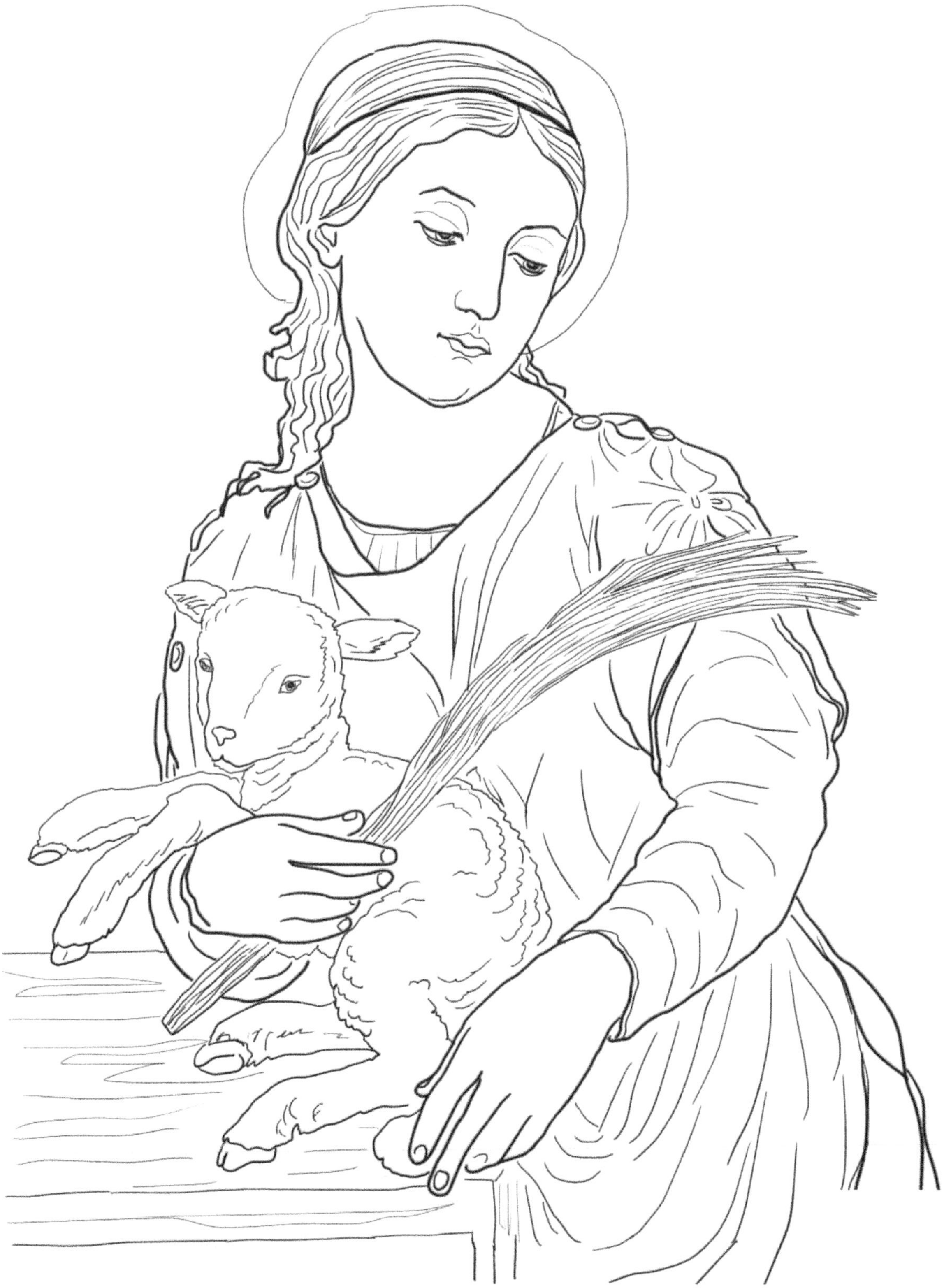

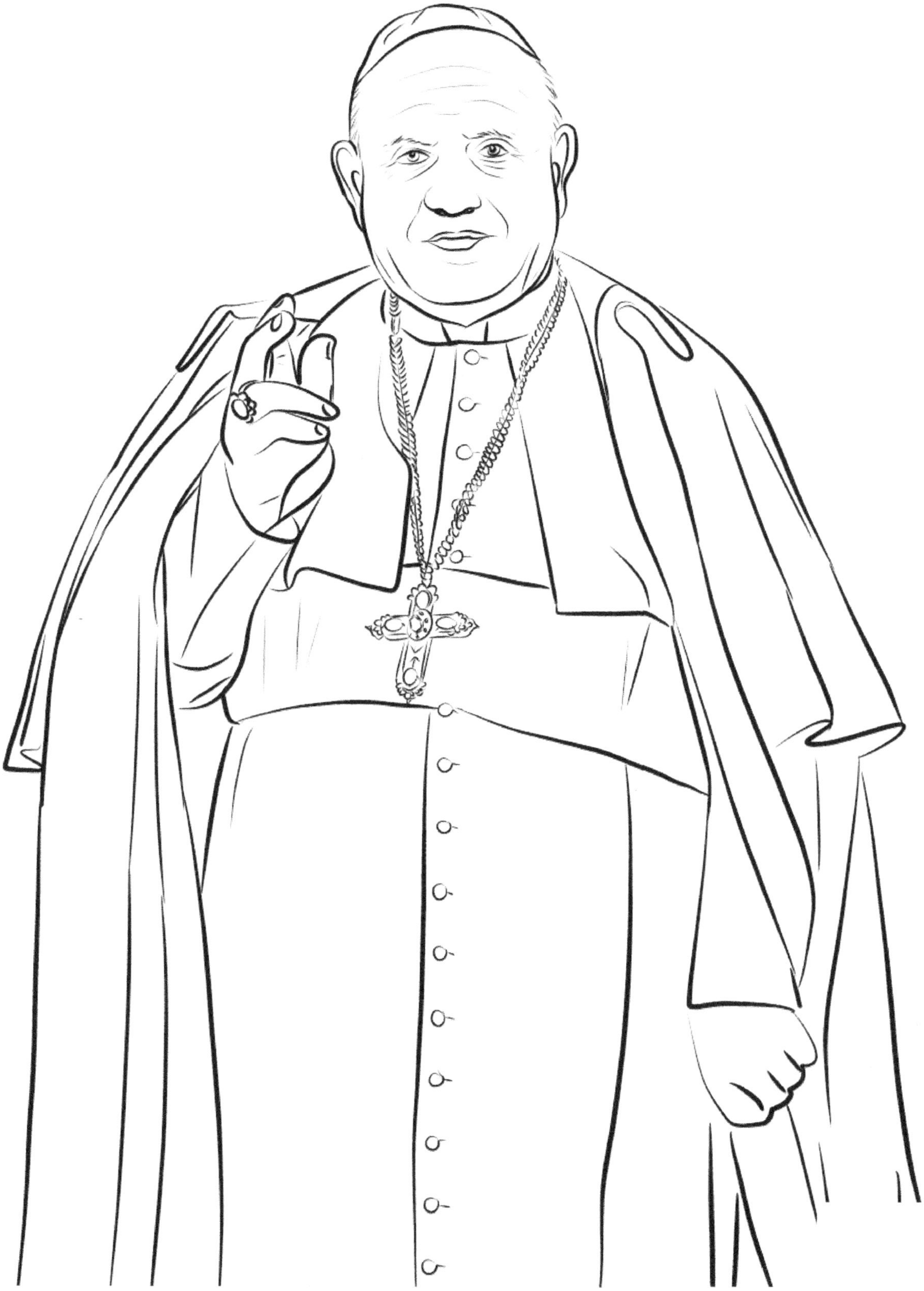

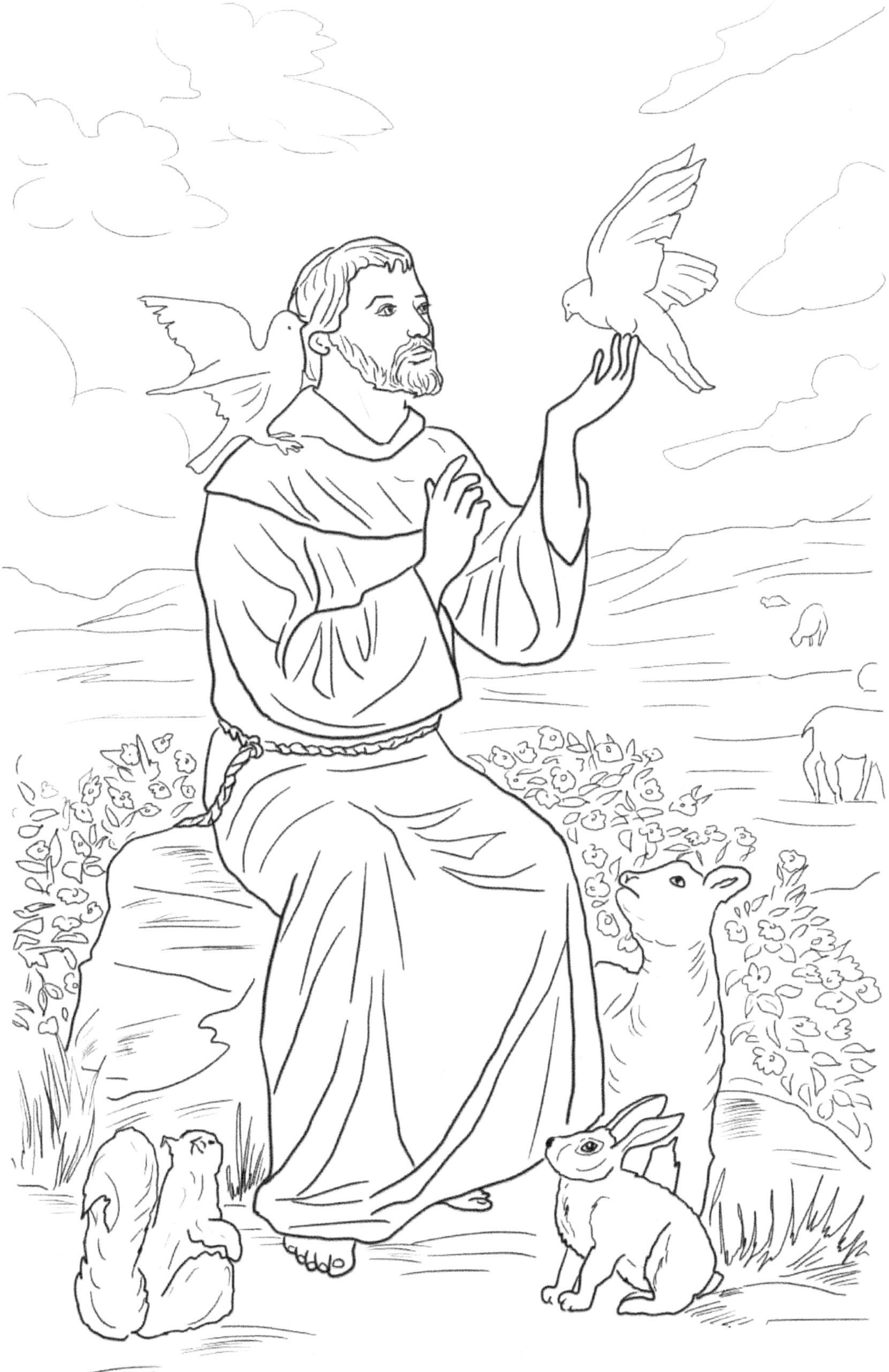

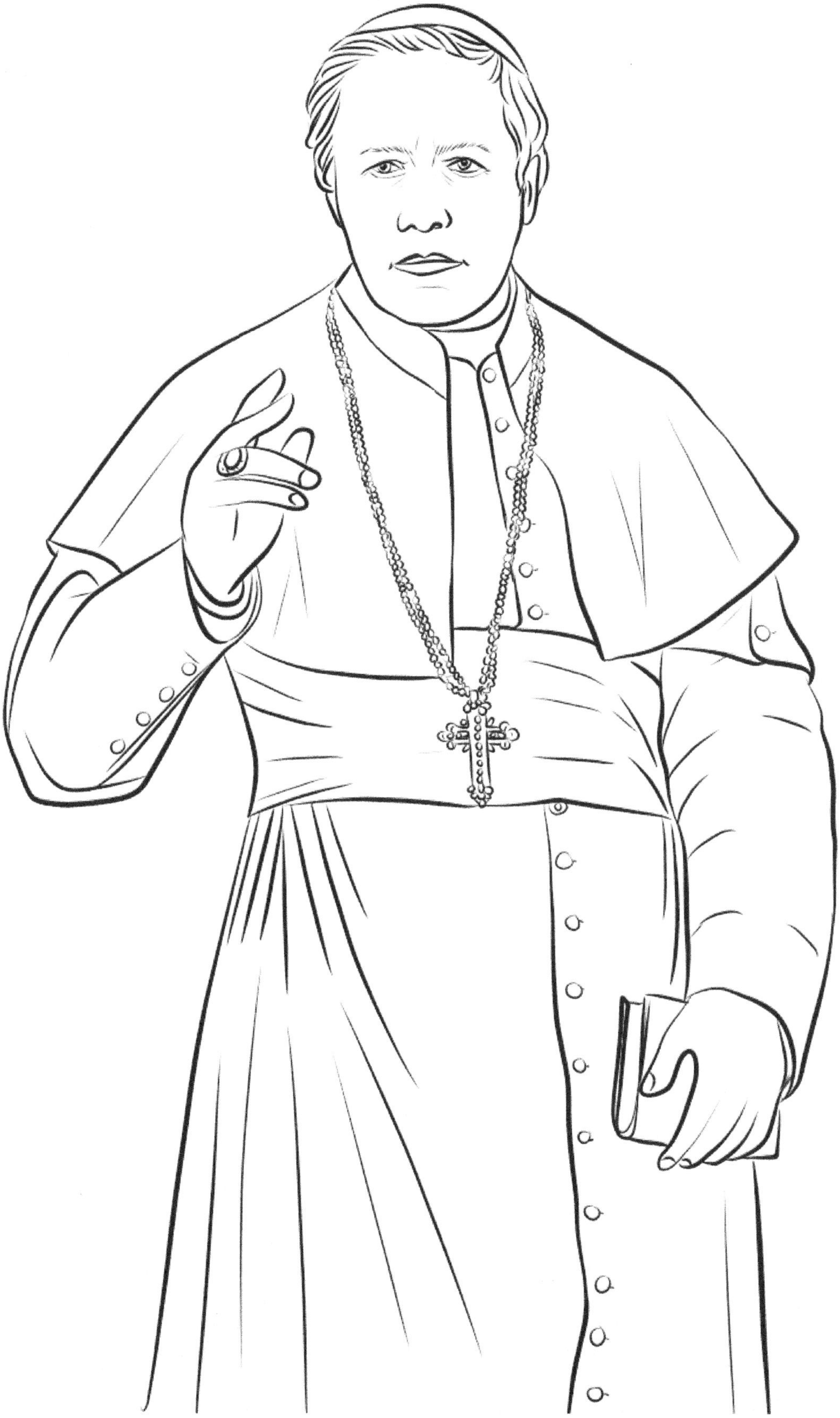

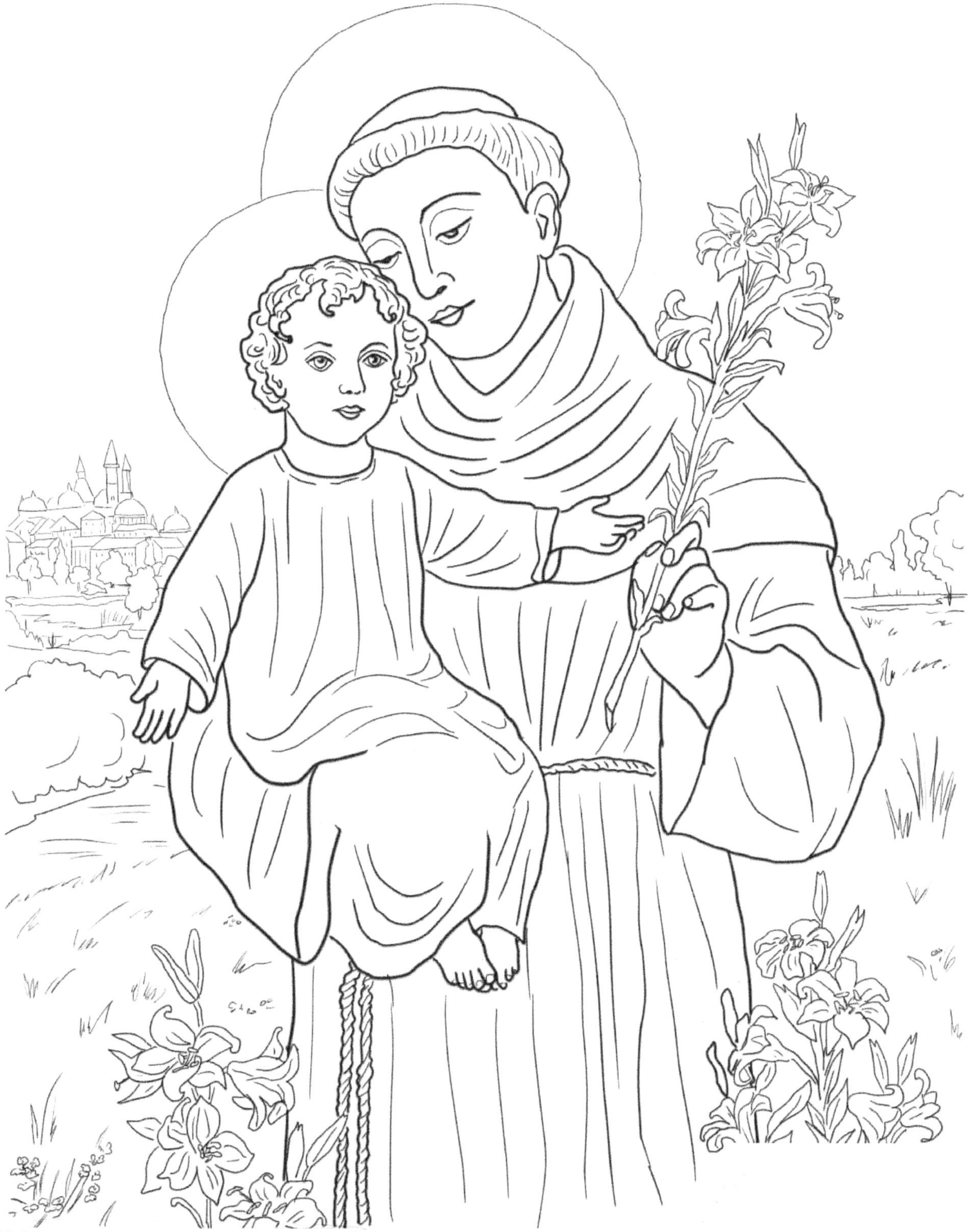

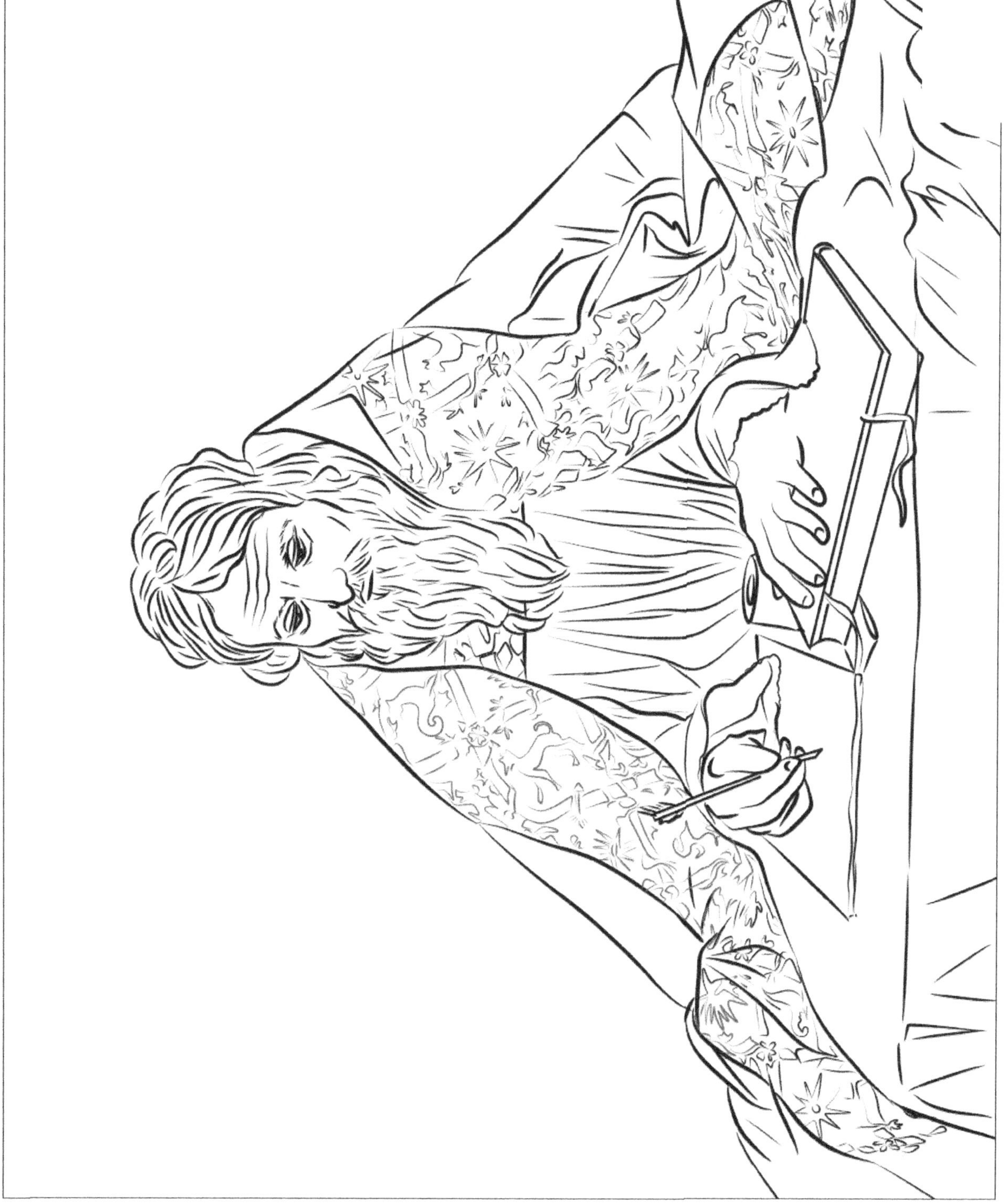

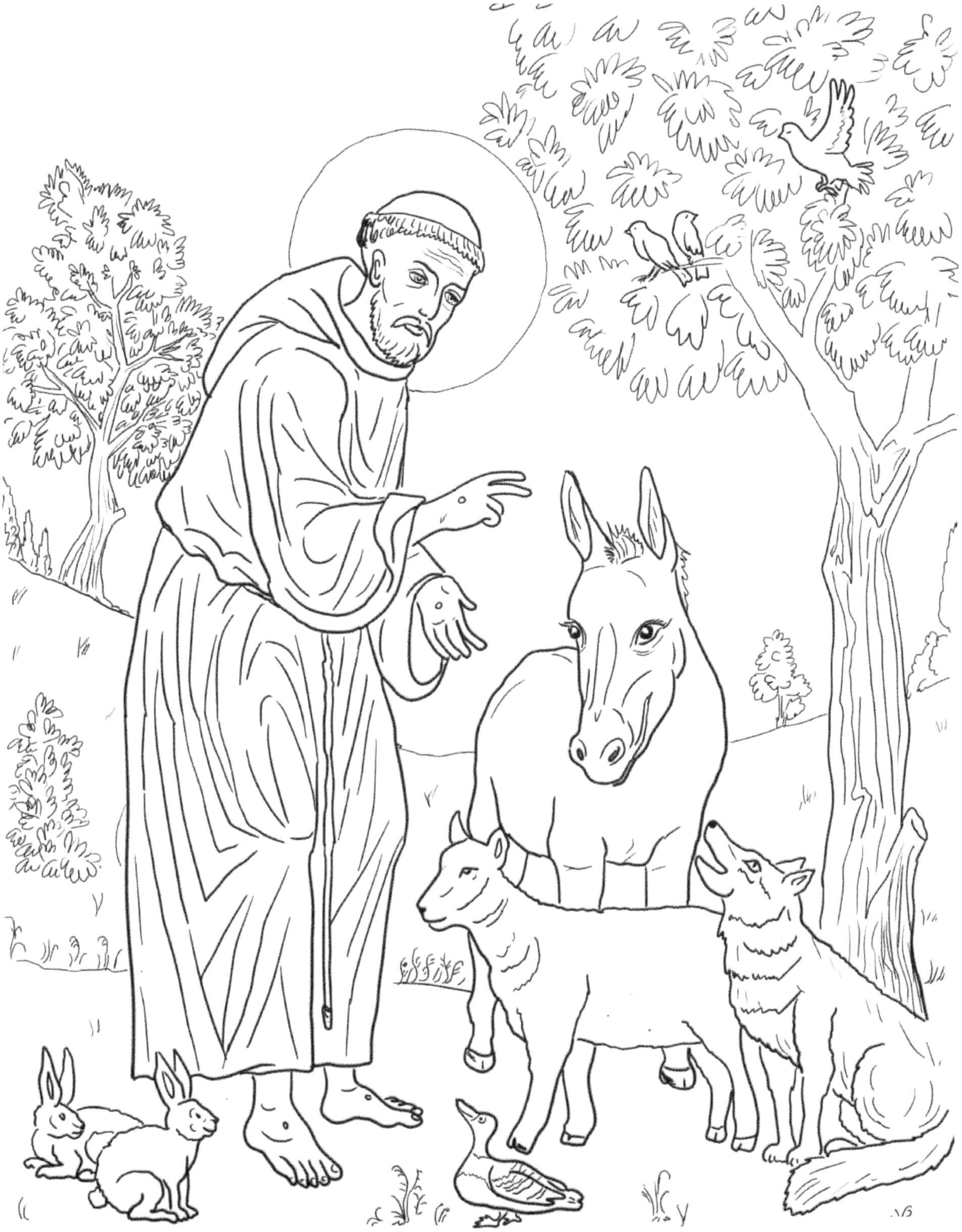

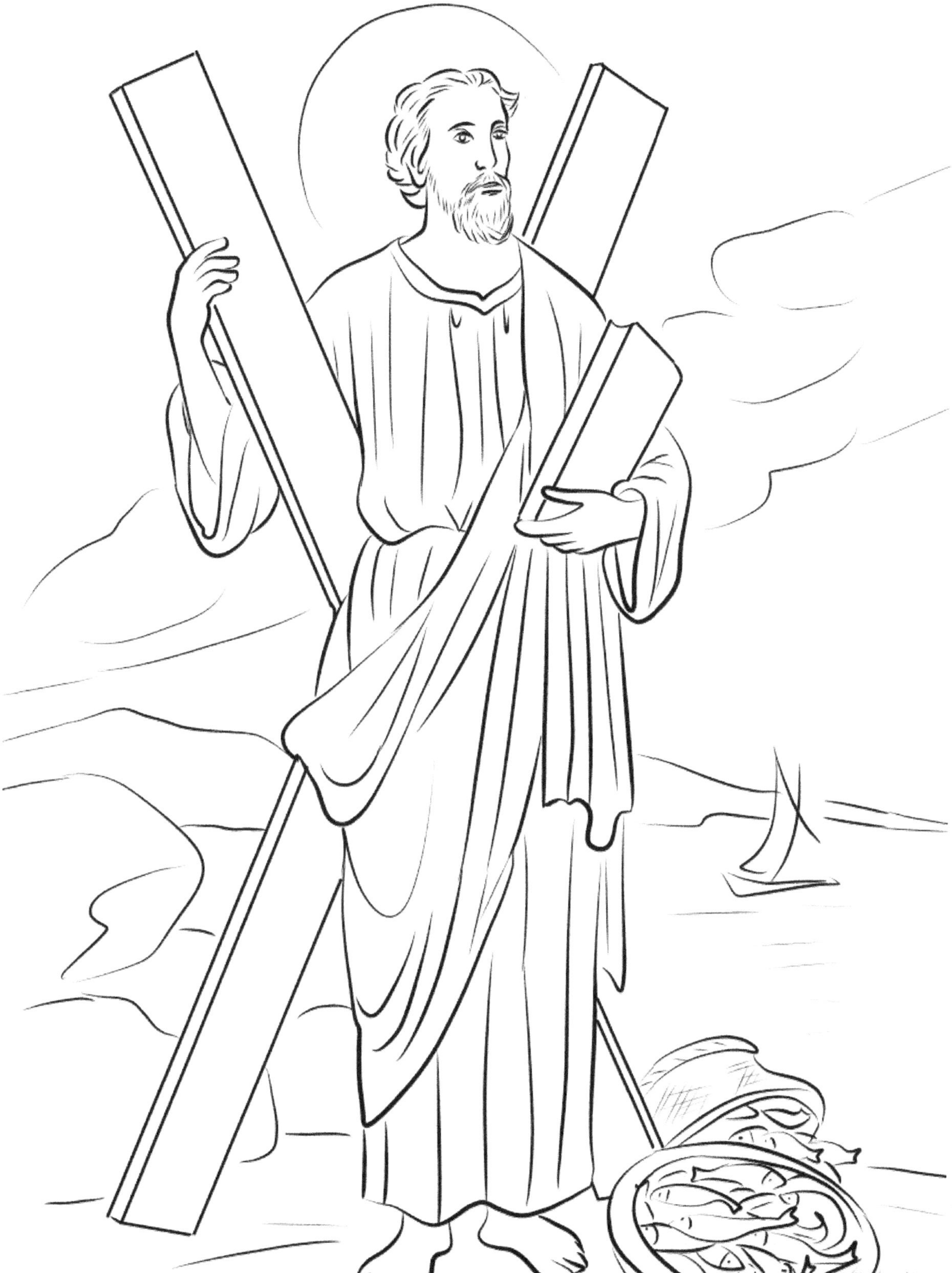

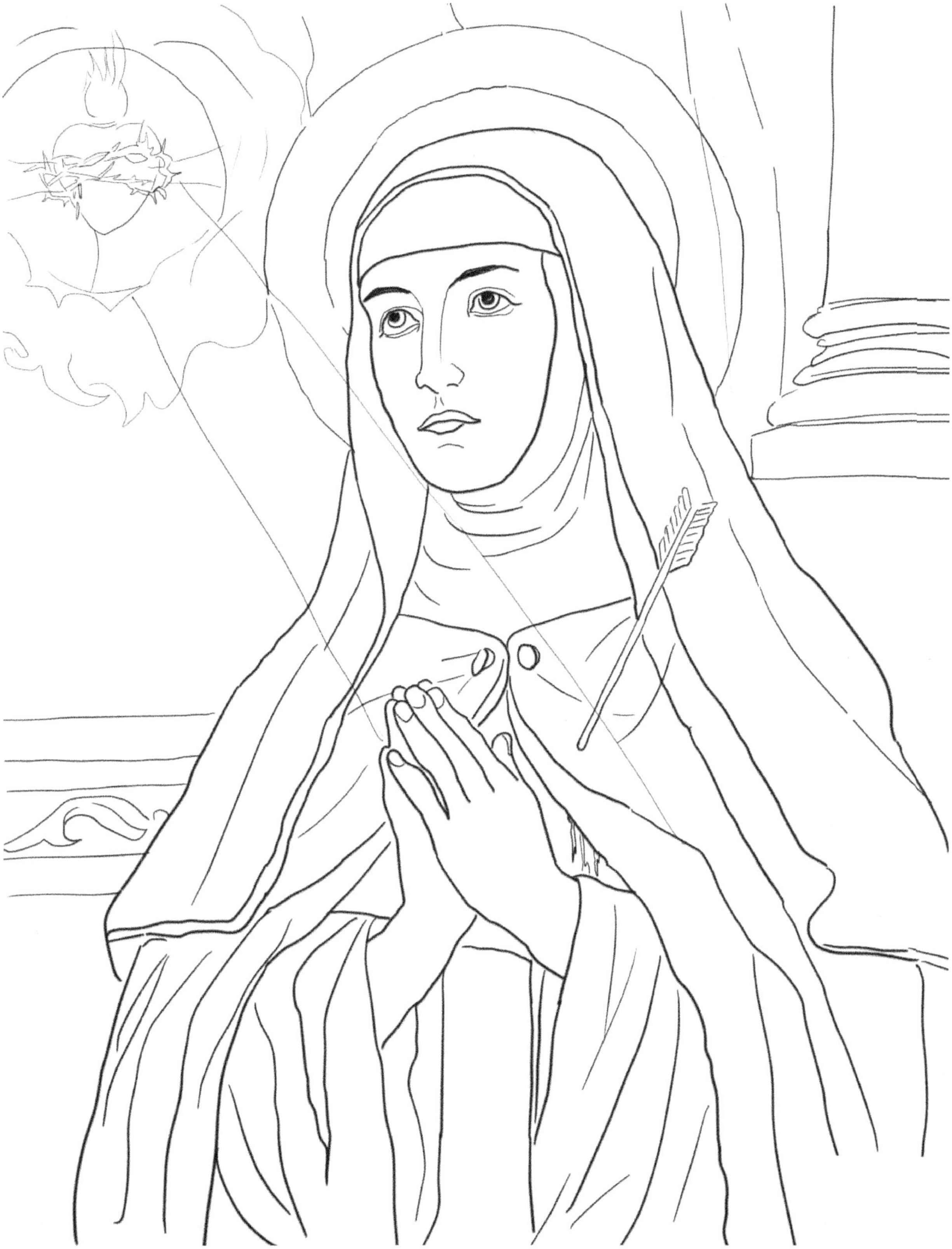

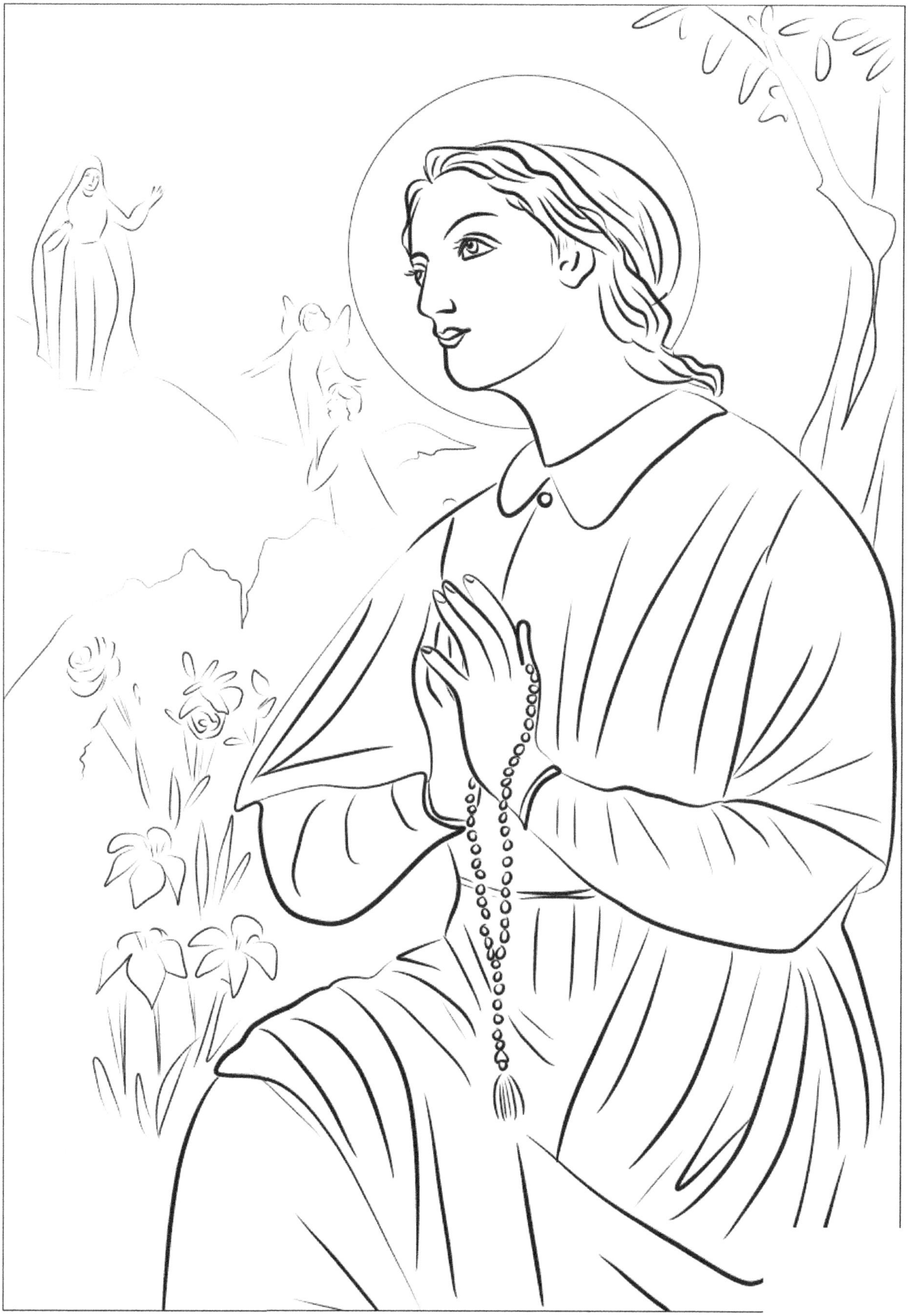

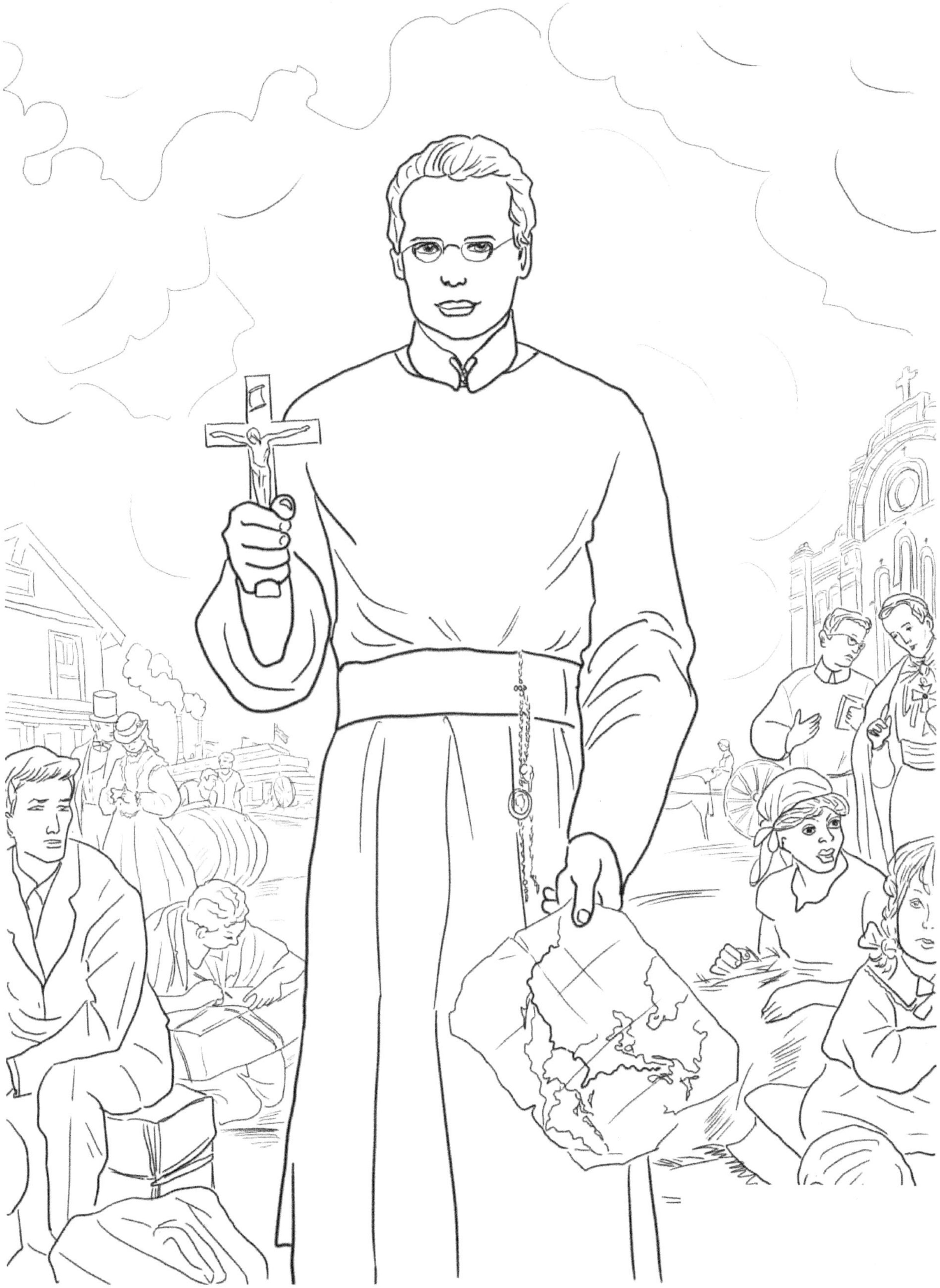

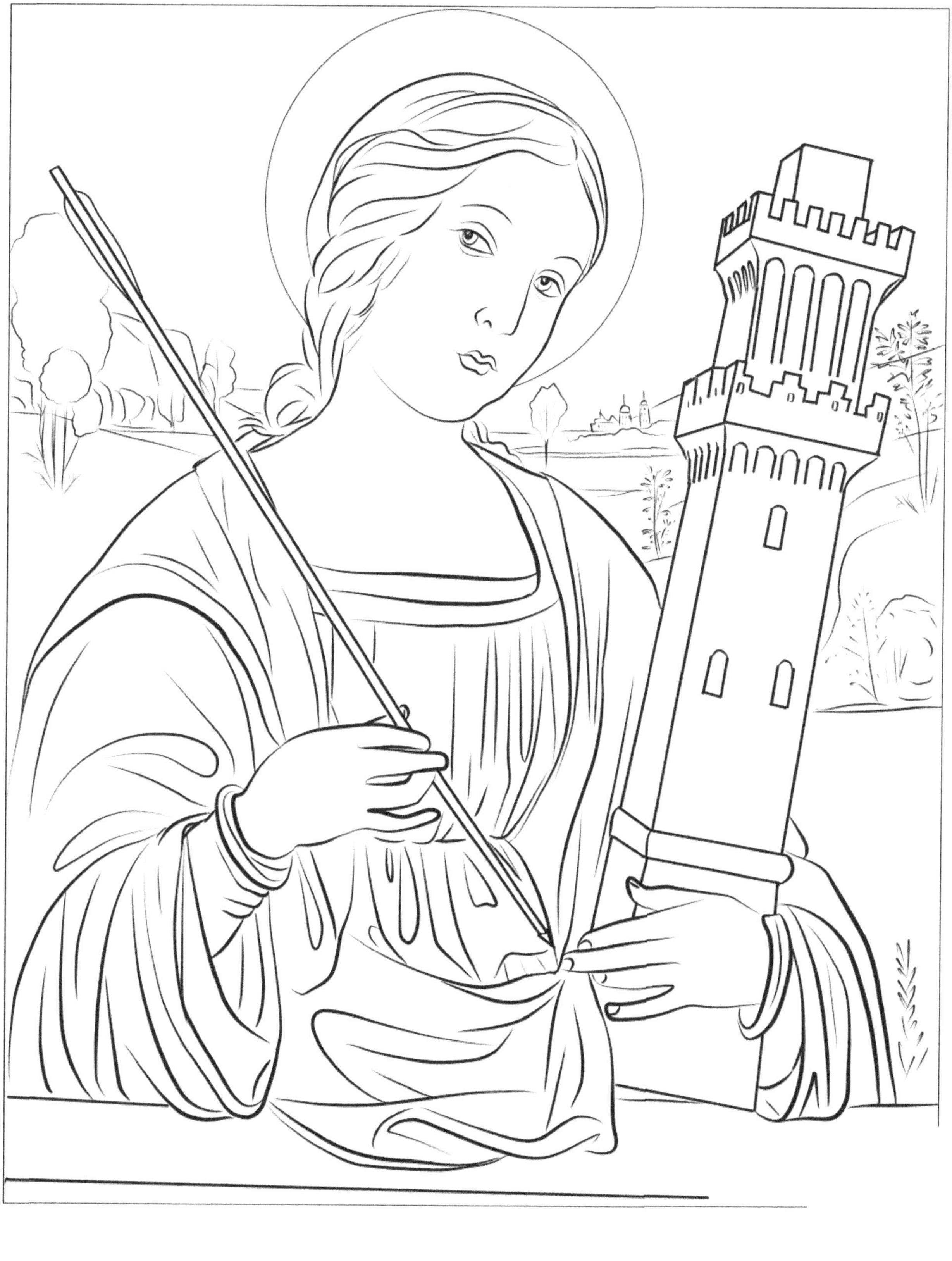

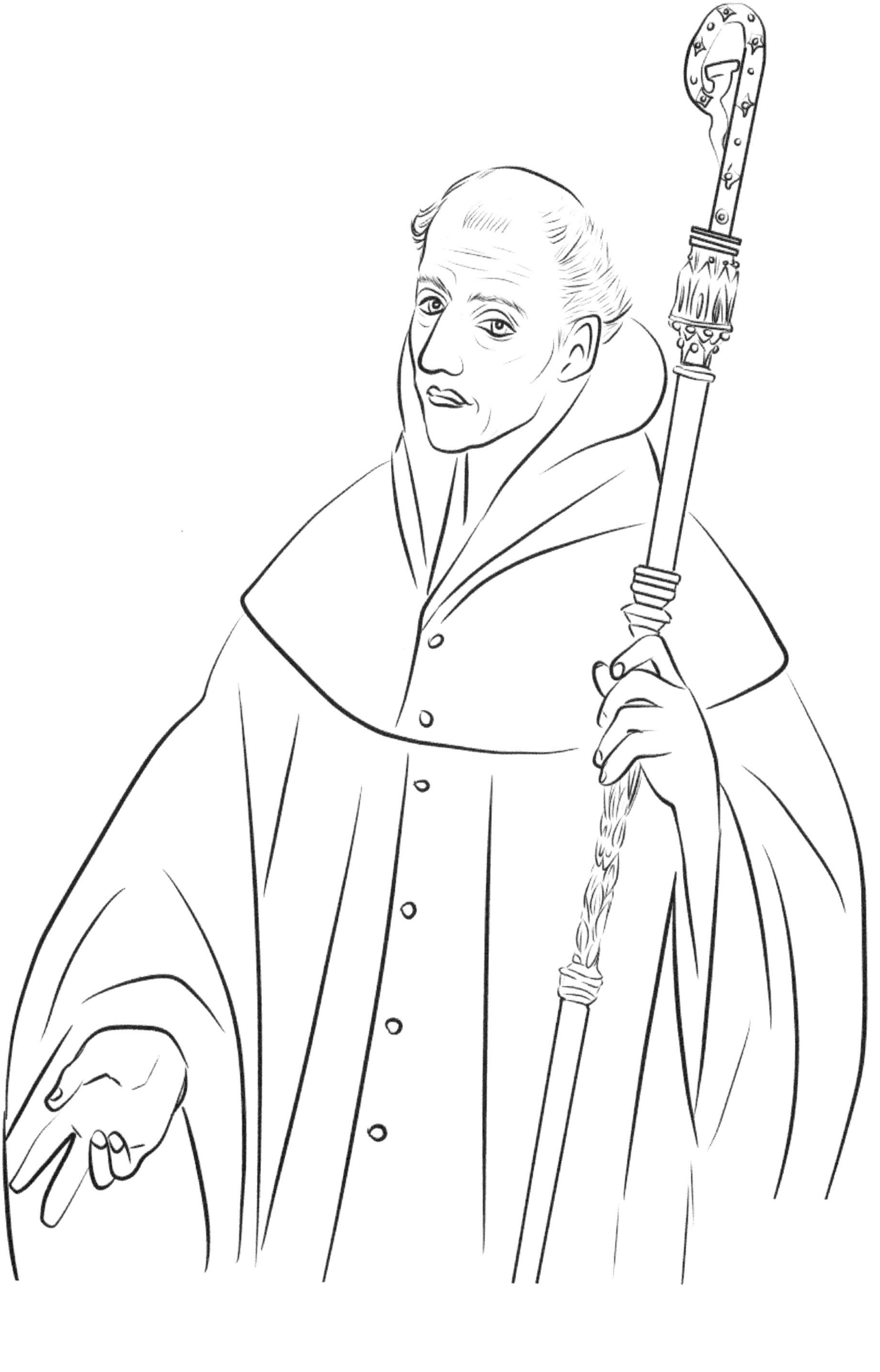

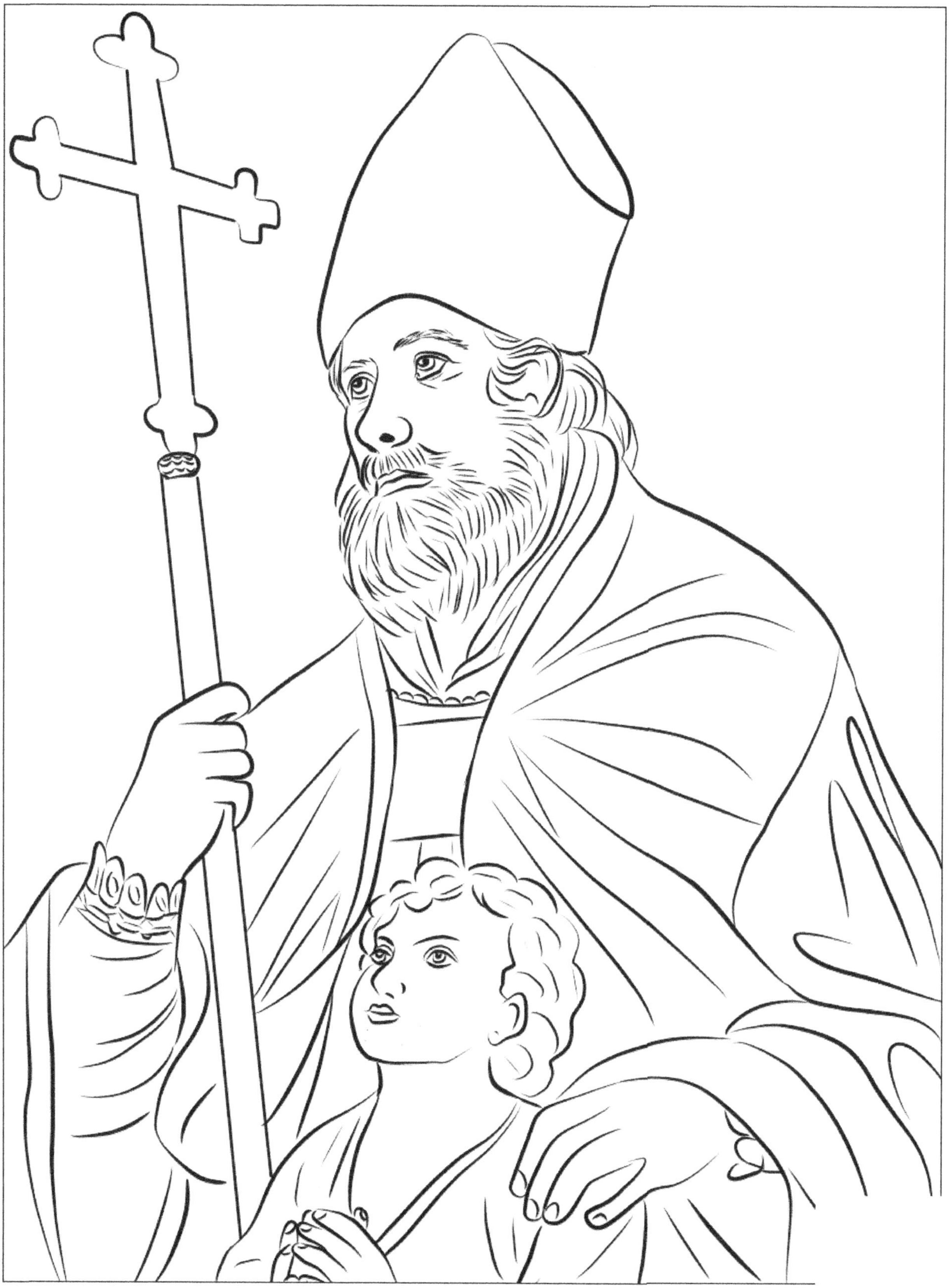

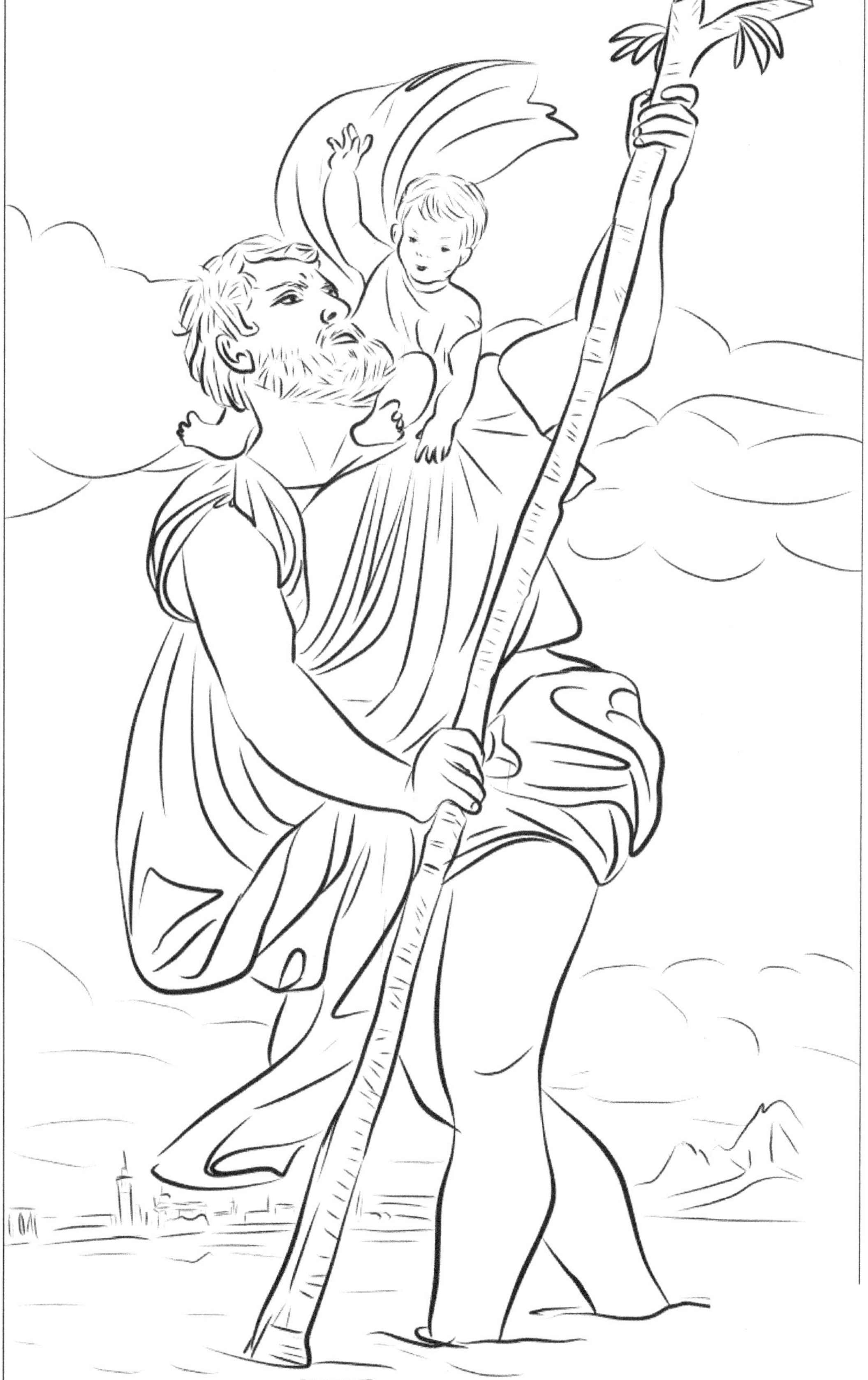

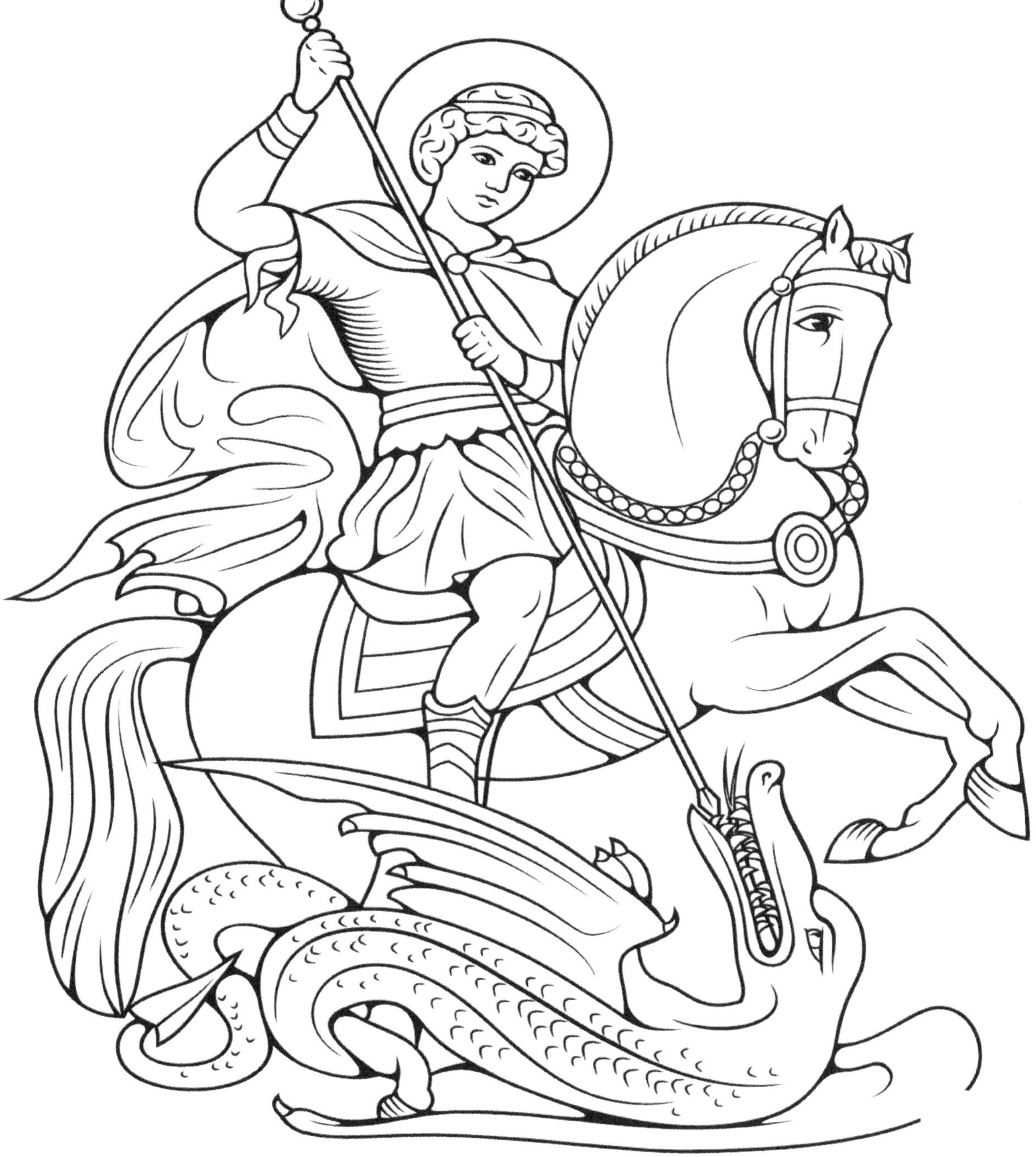

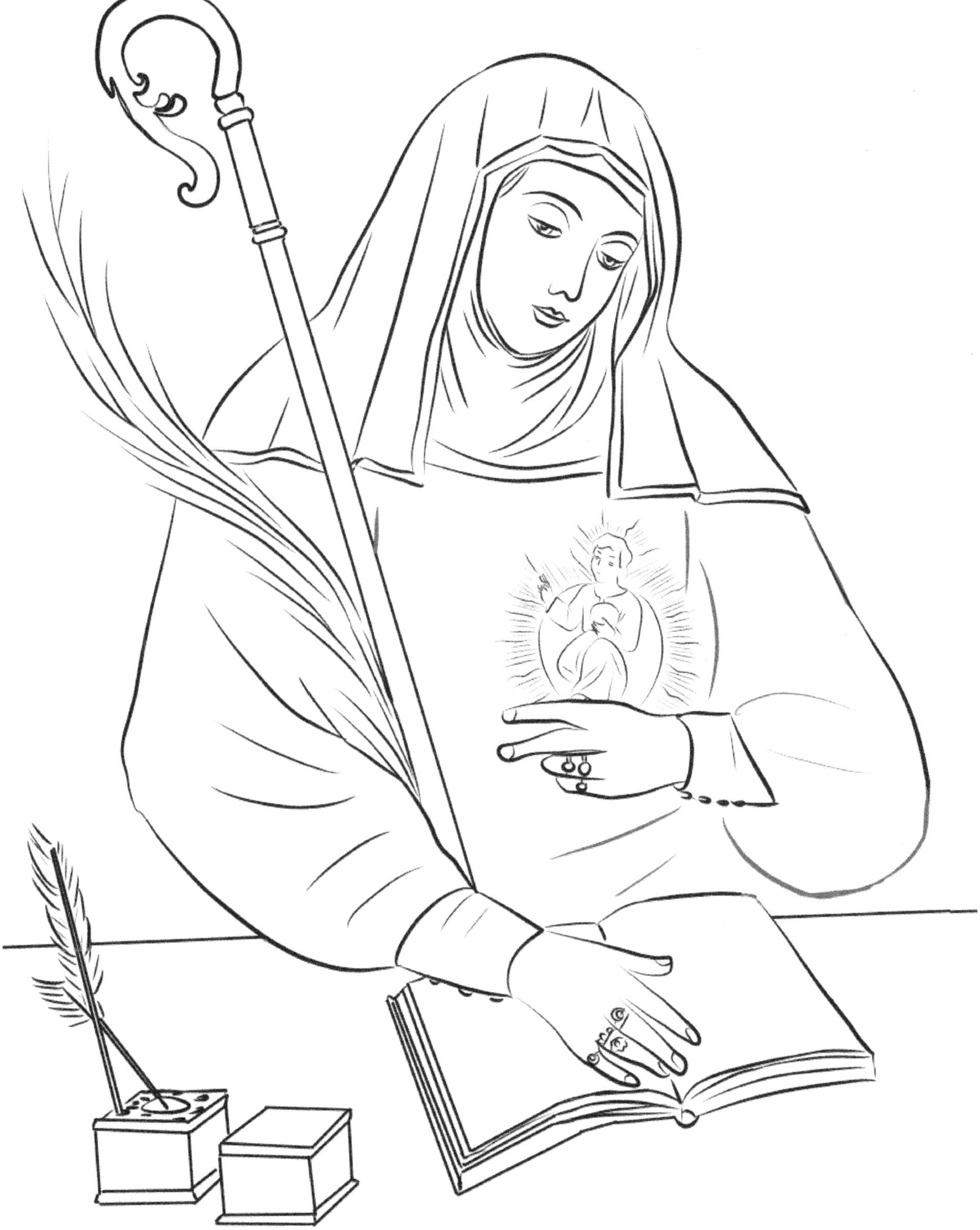

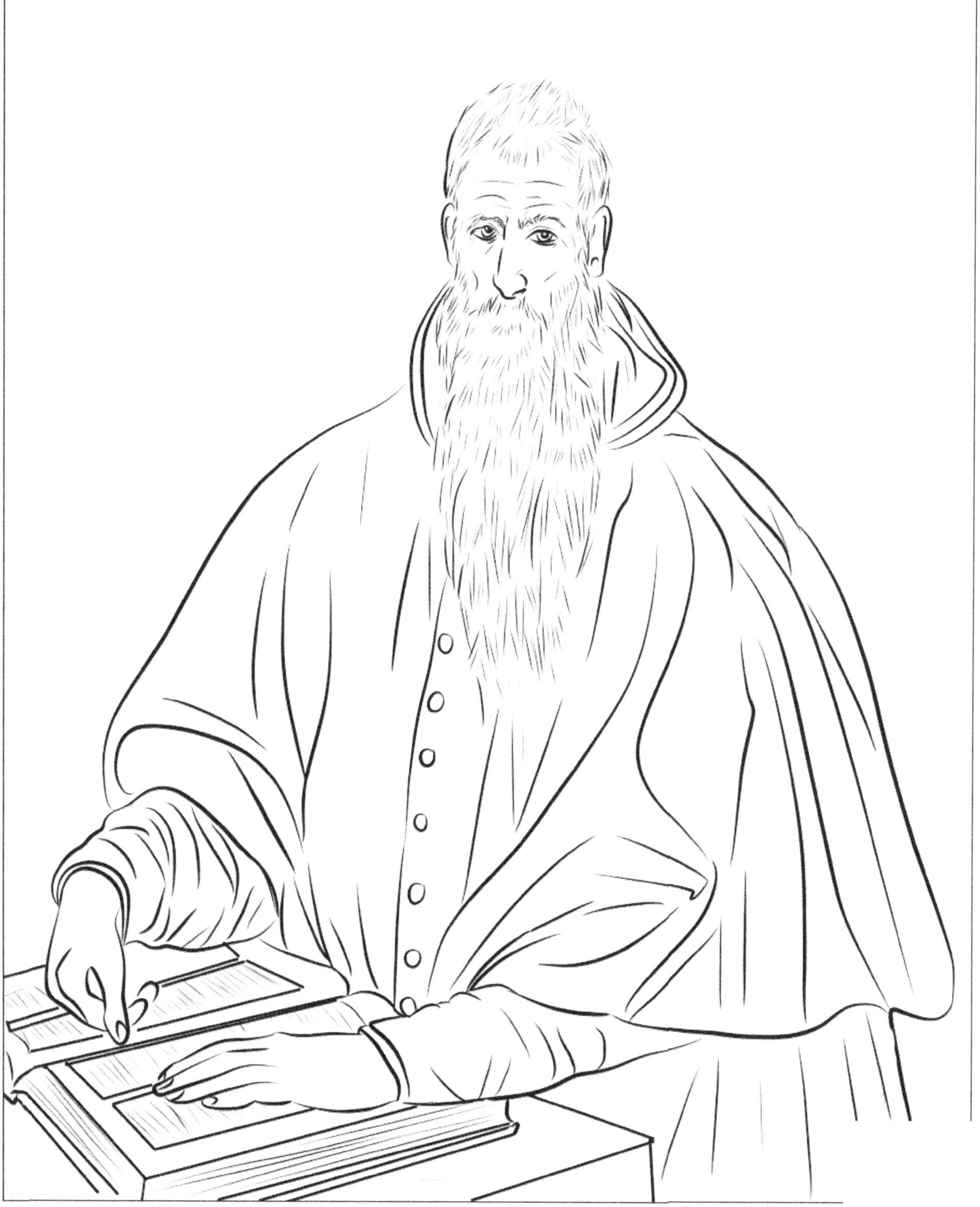

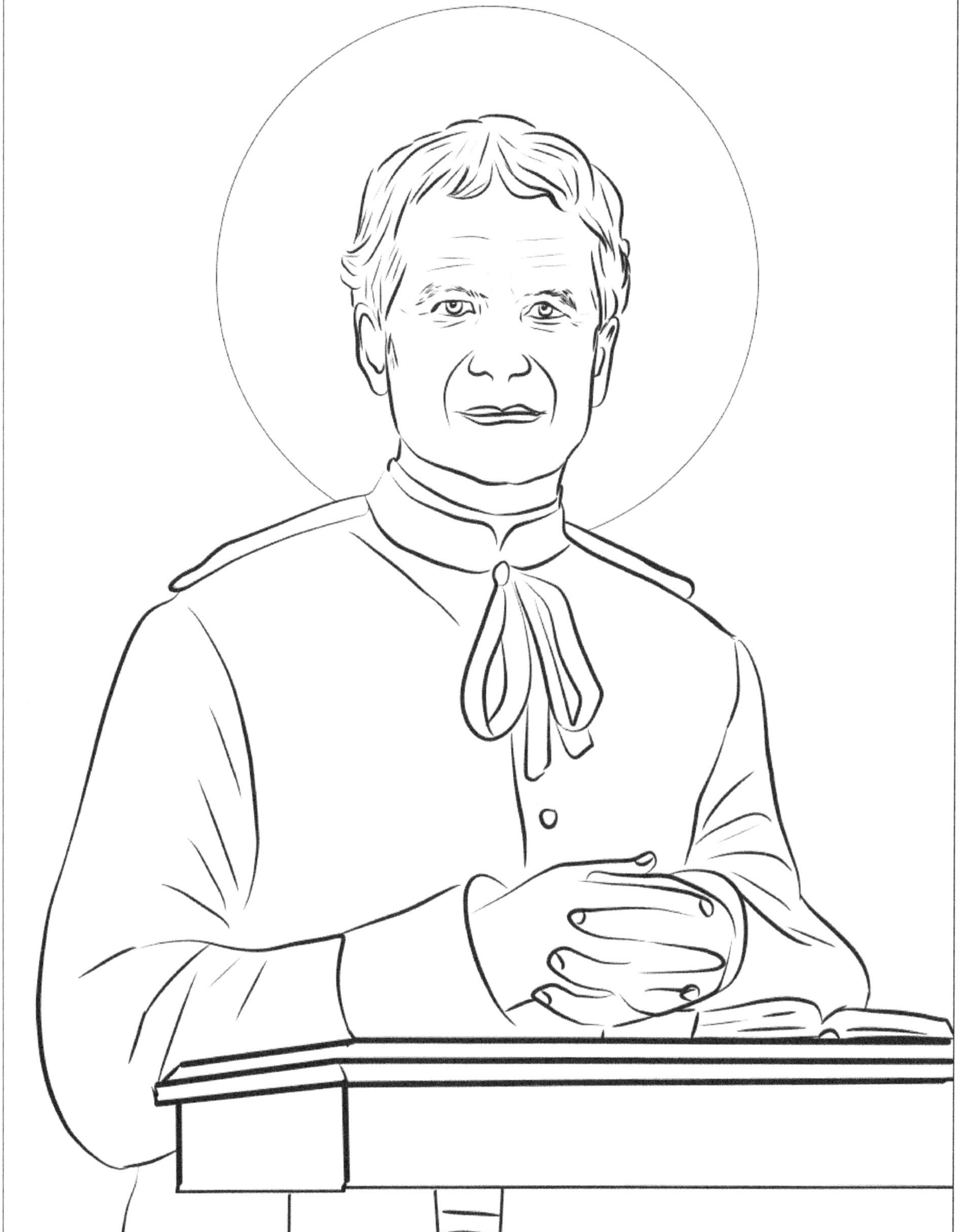

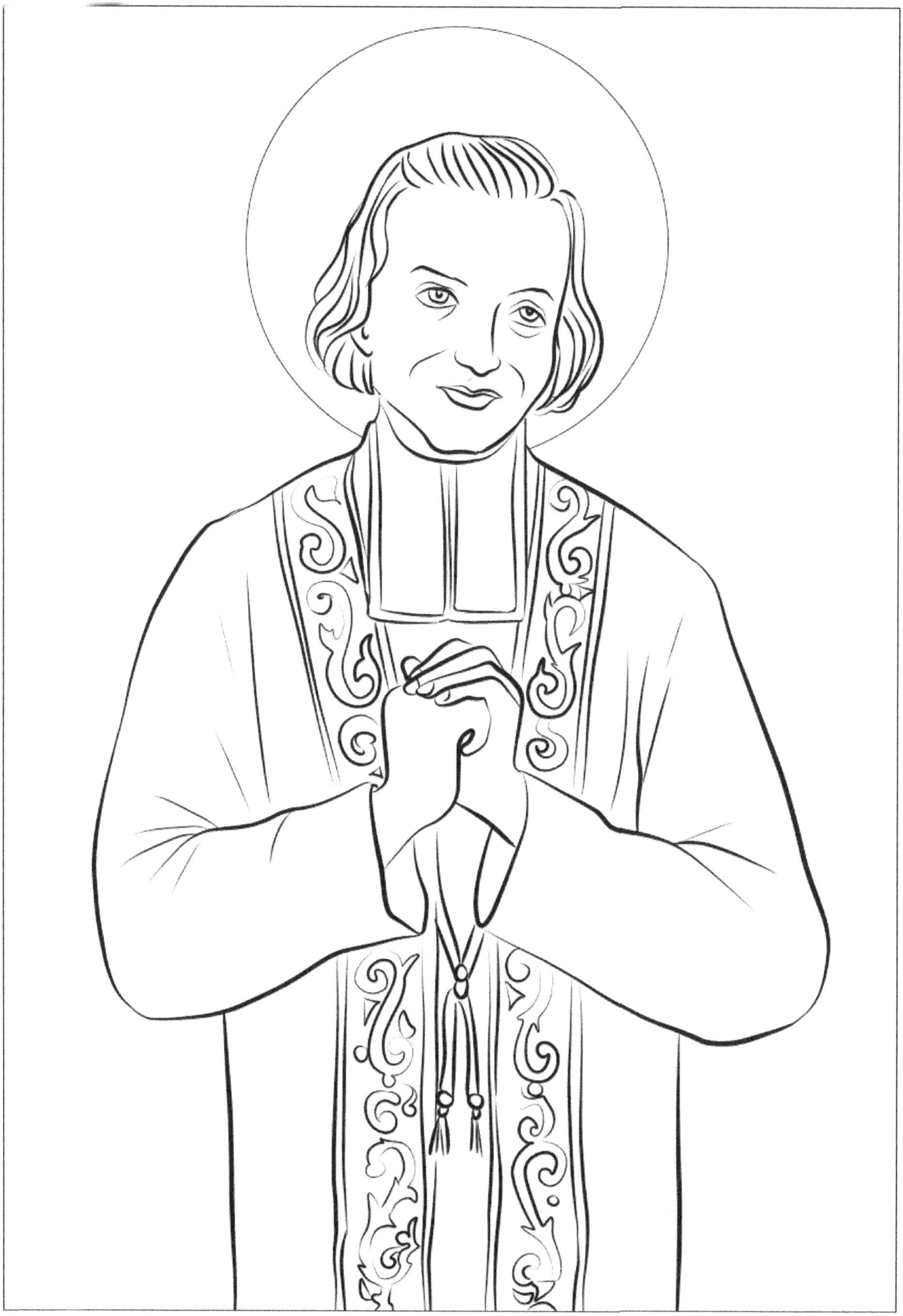

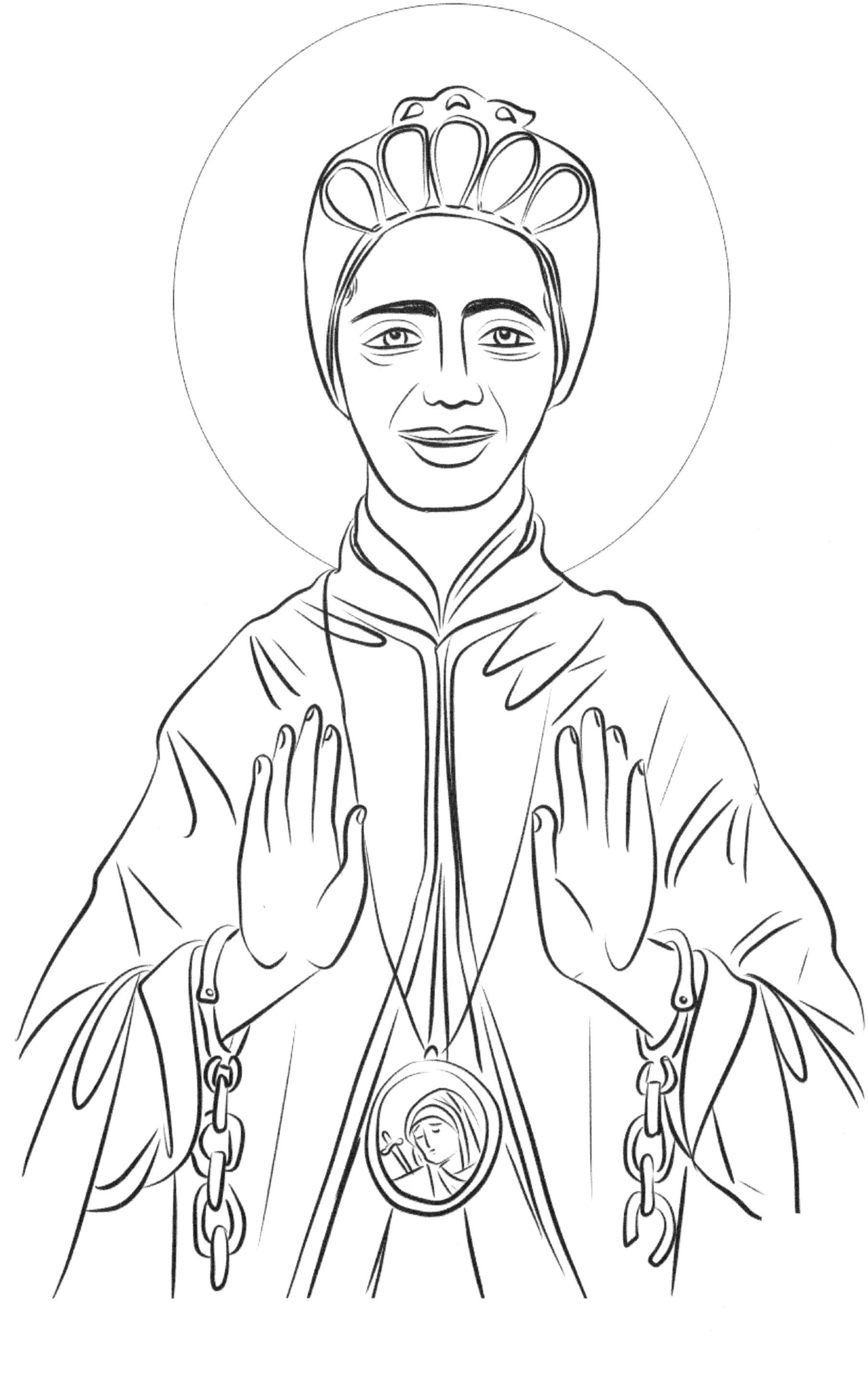

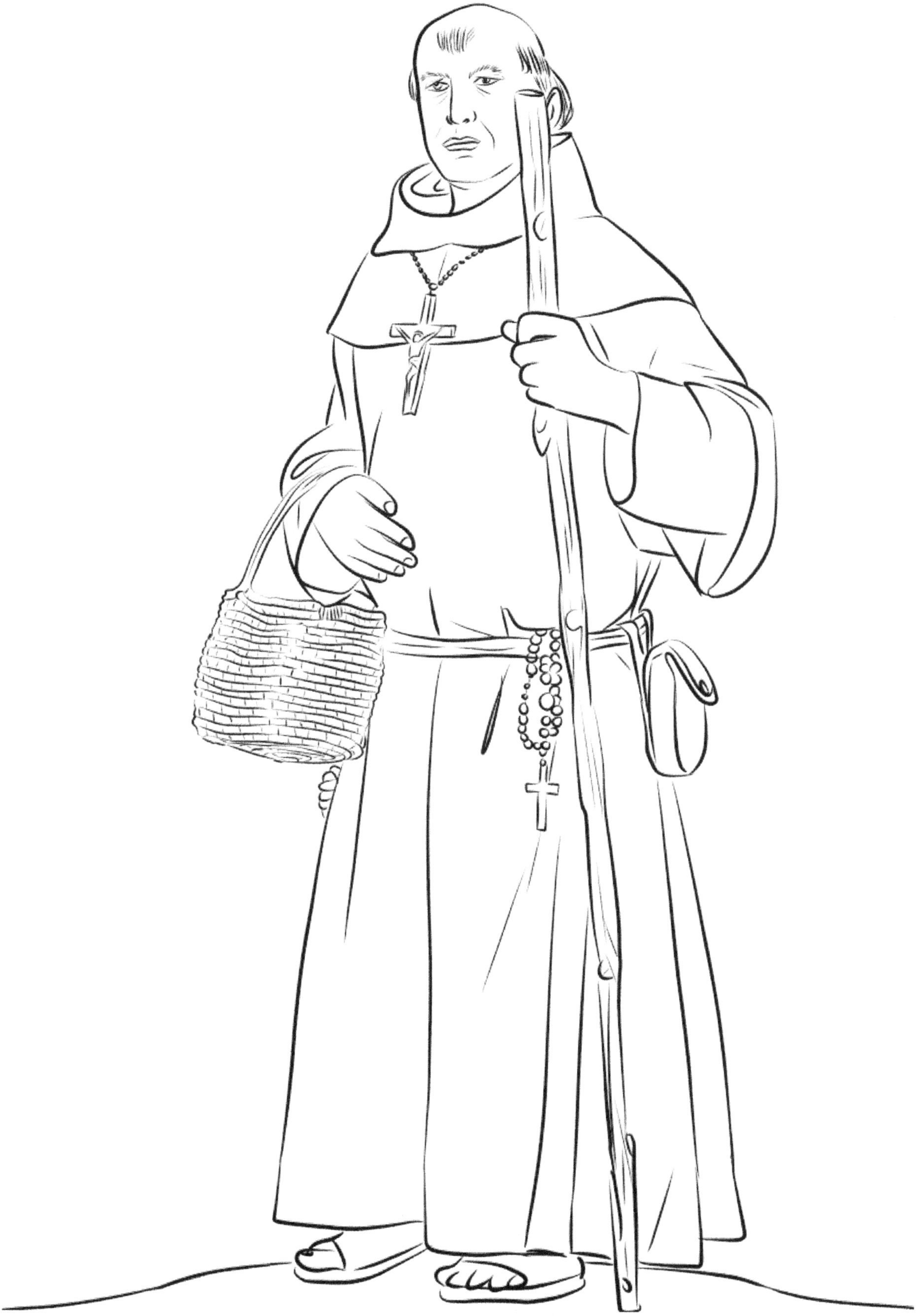

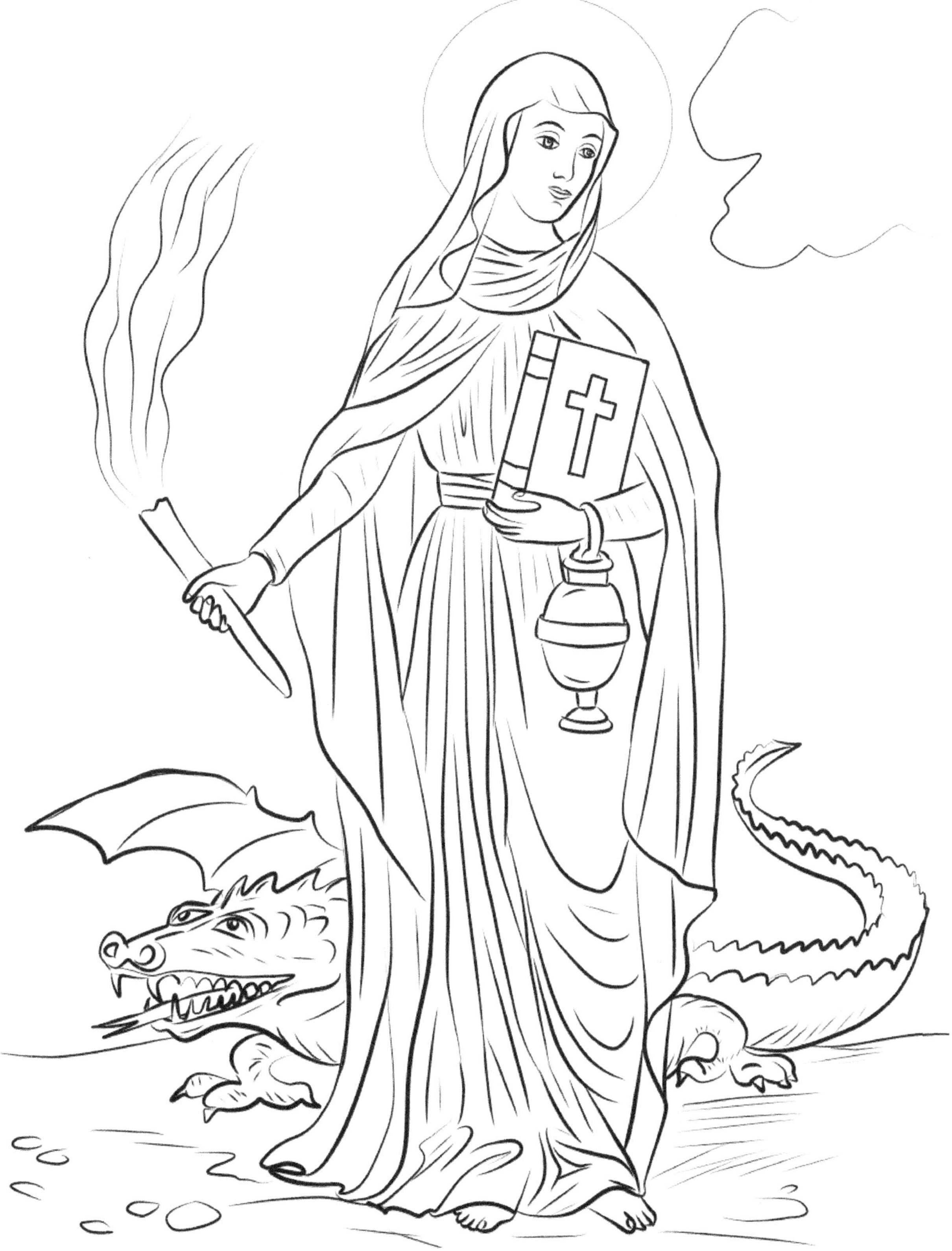

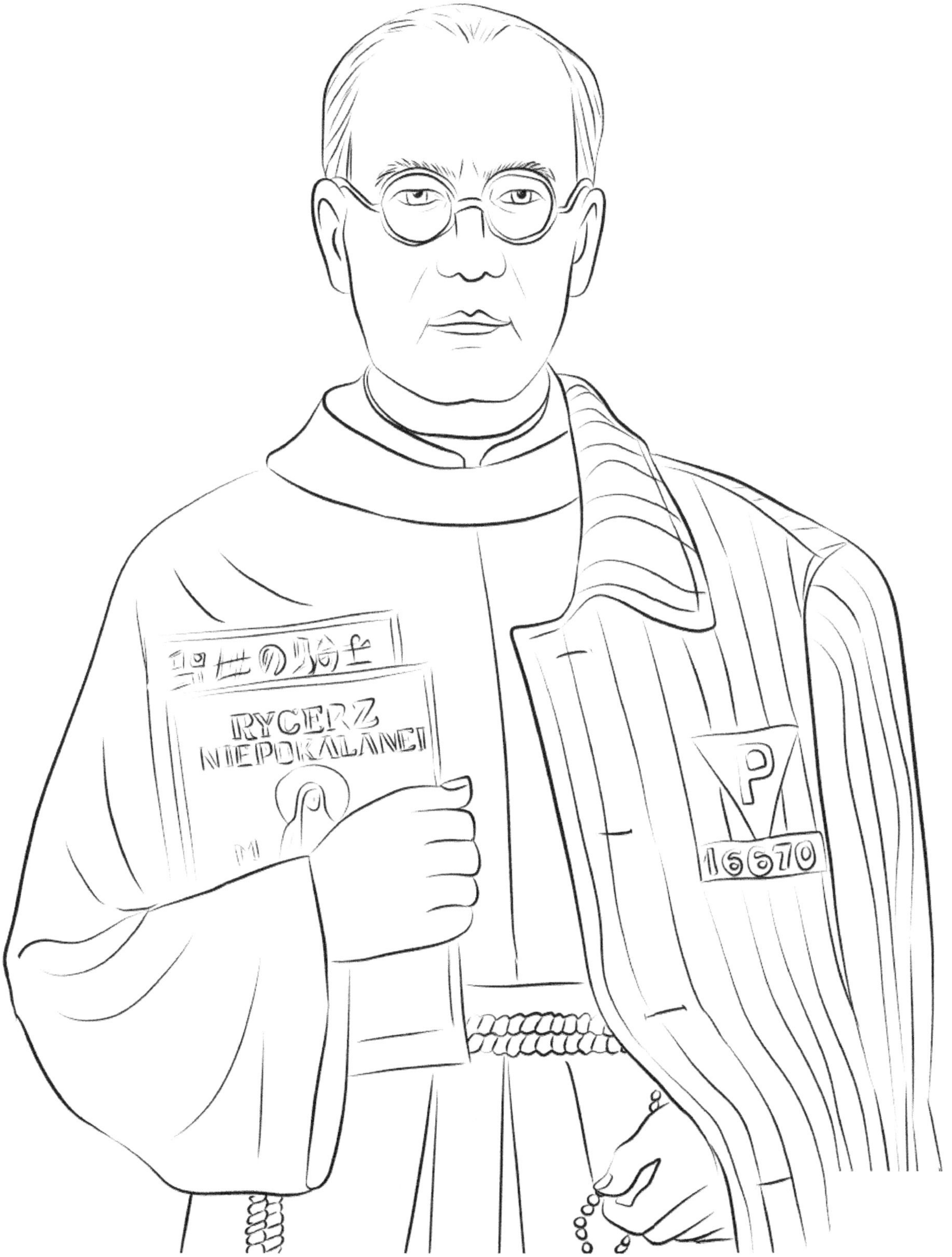
RYCERZ
P
16670

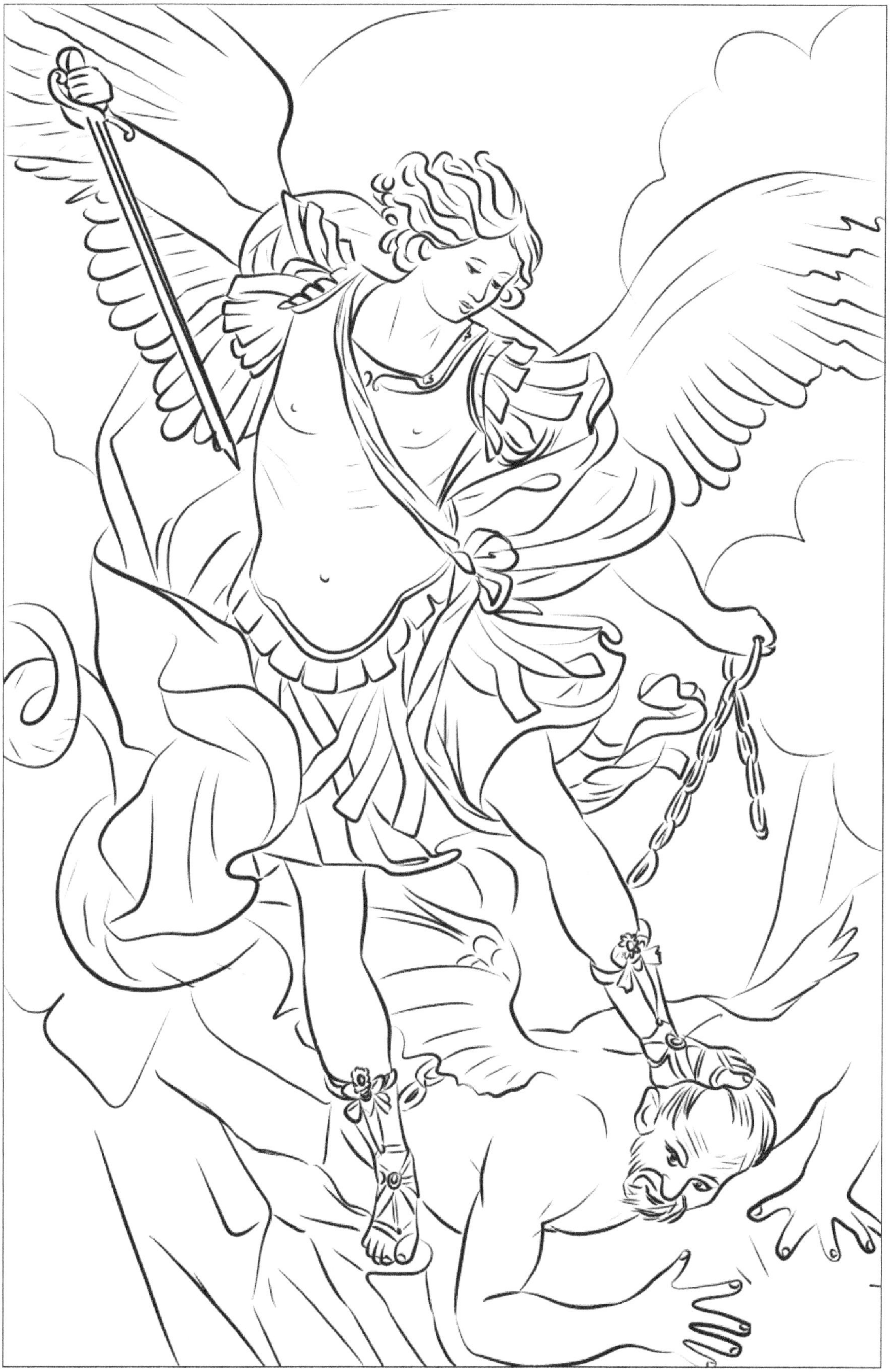

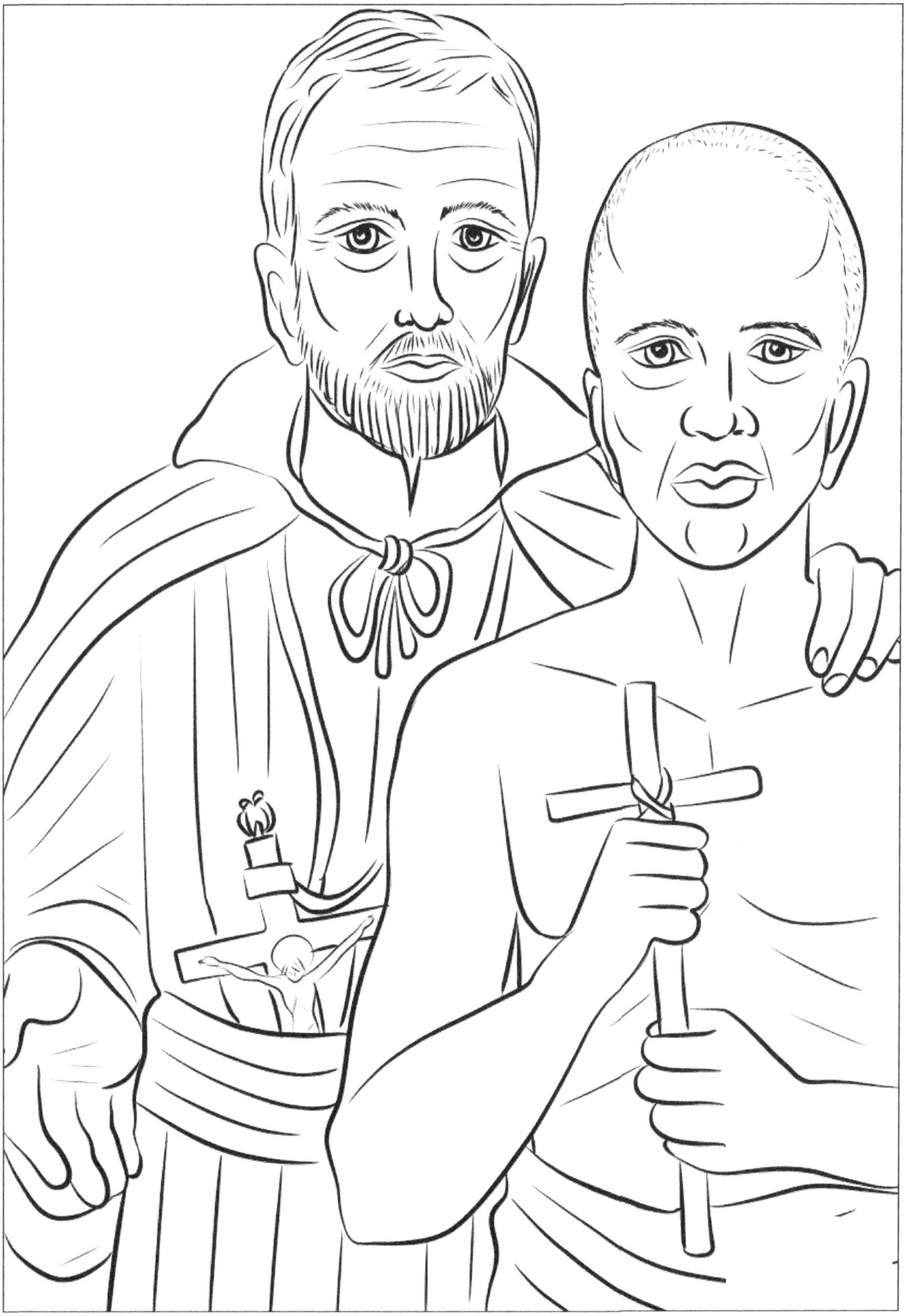

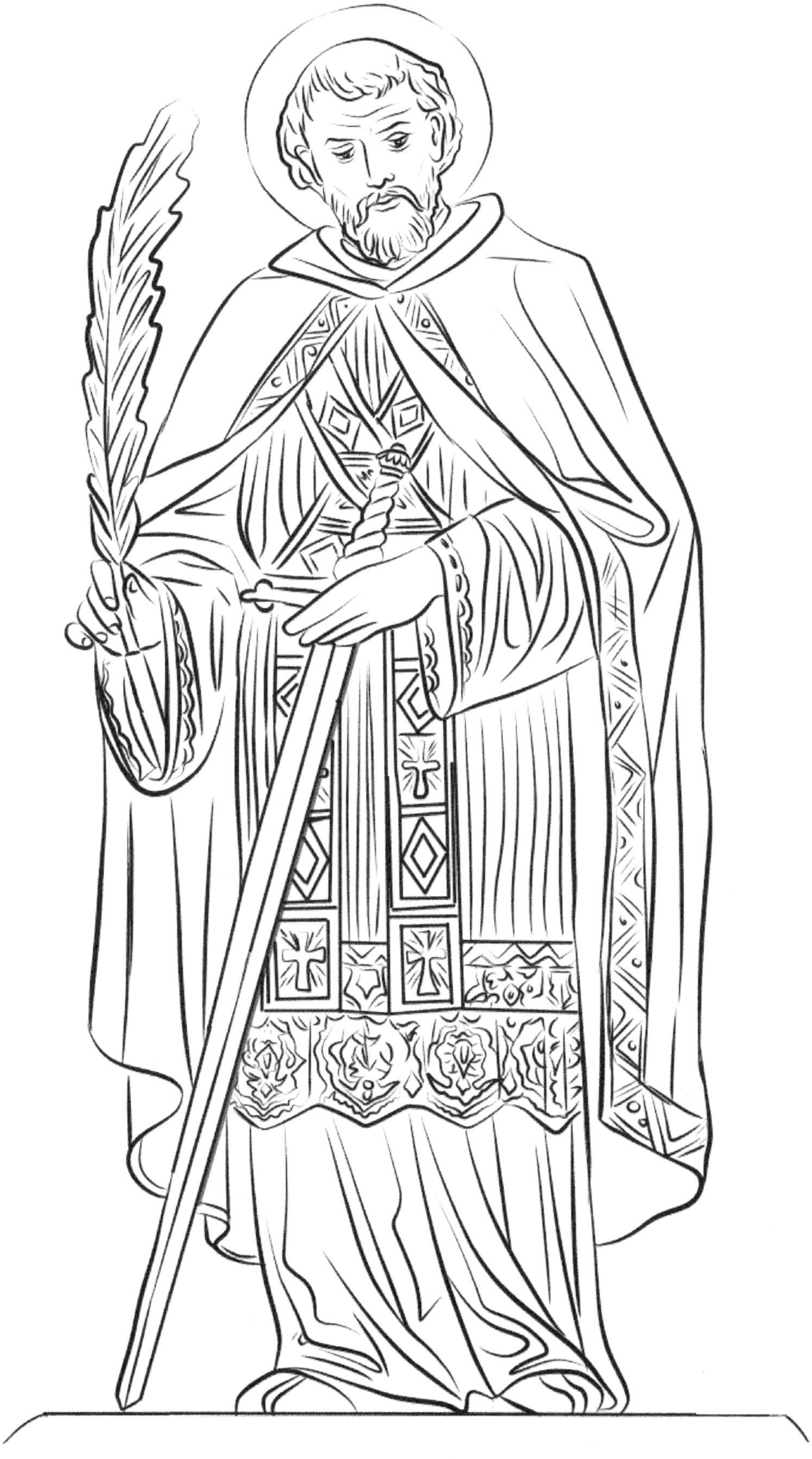

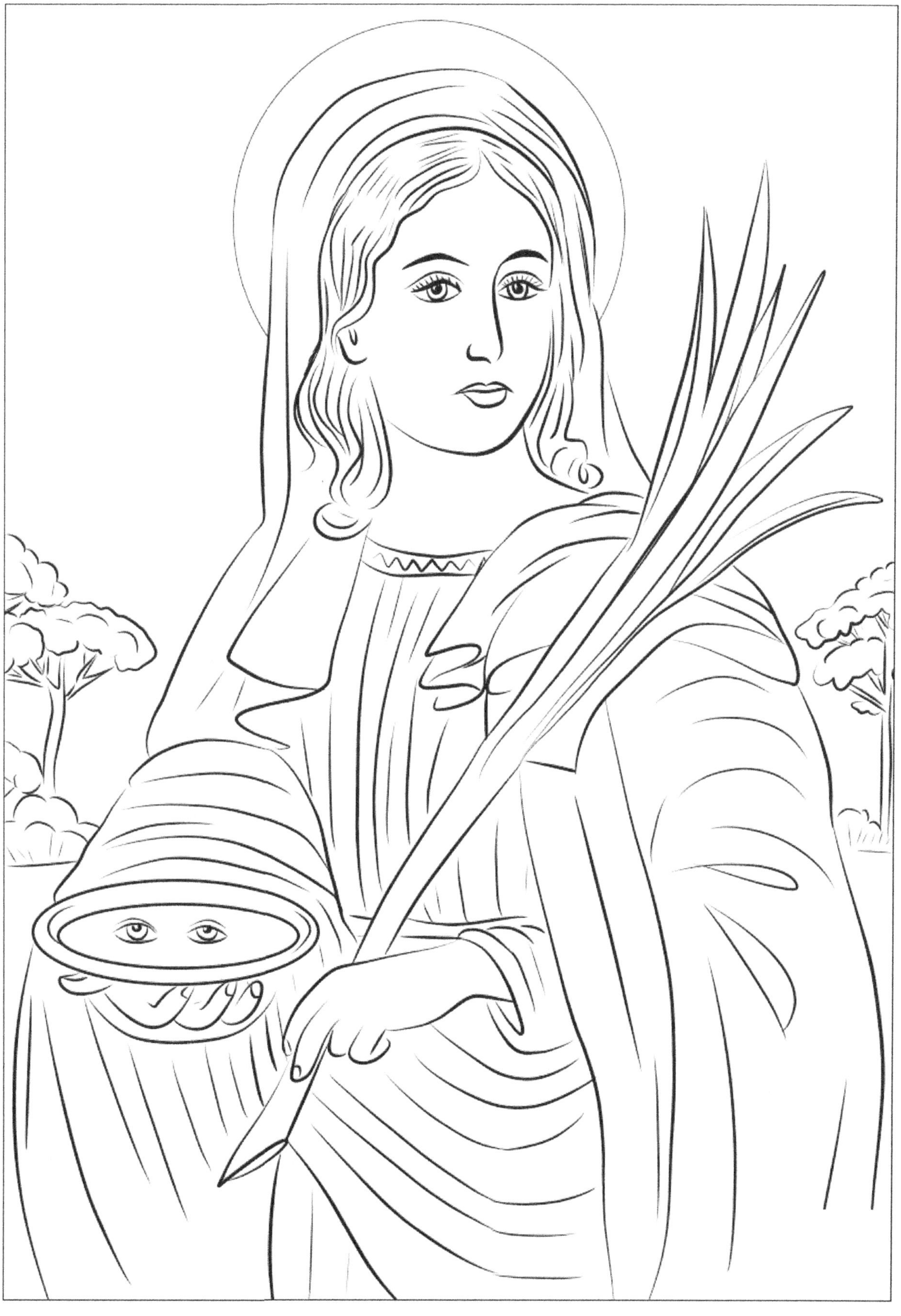

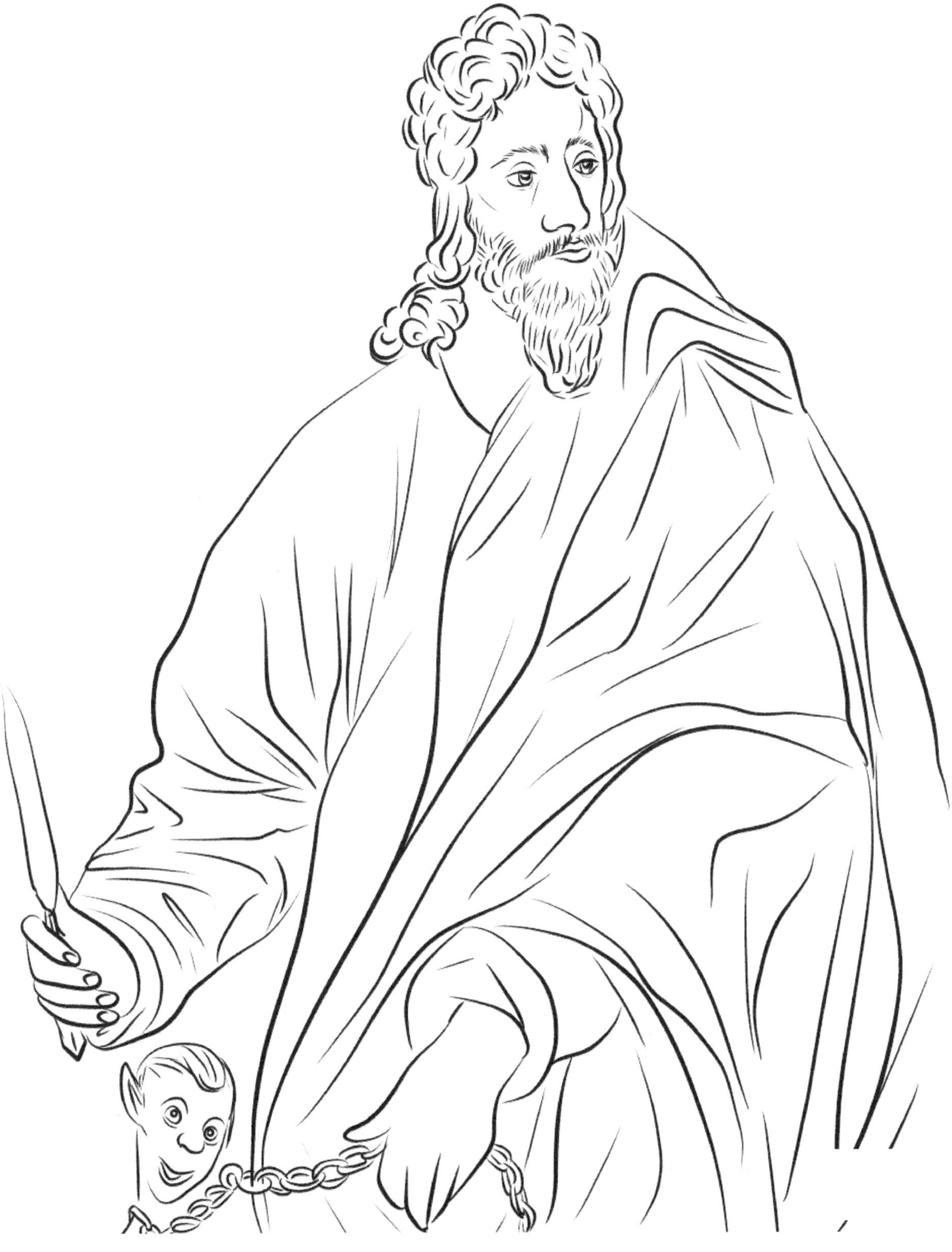

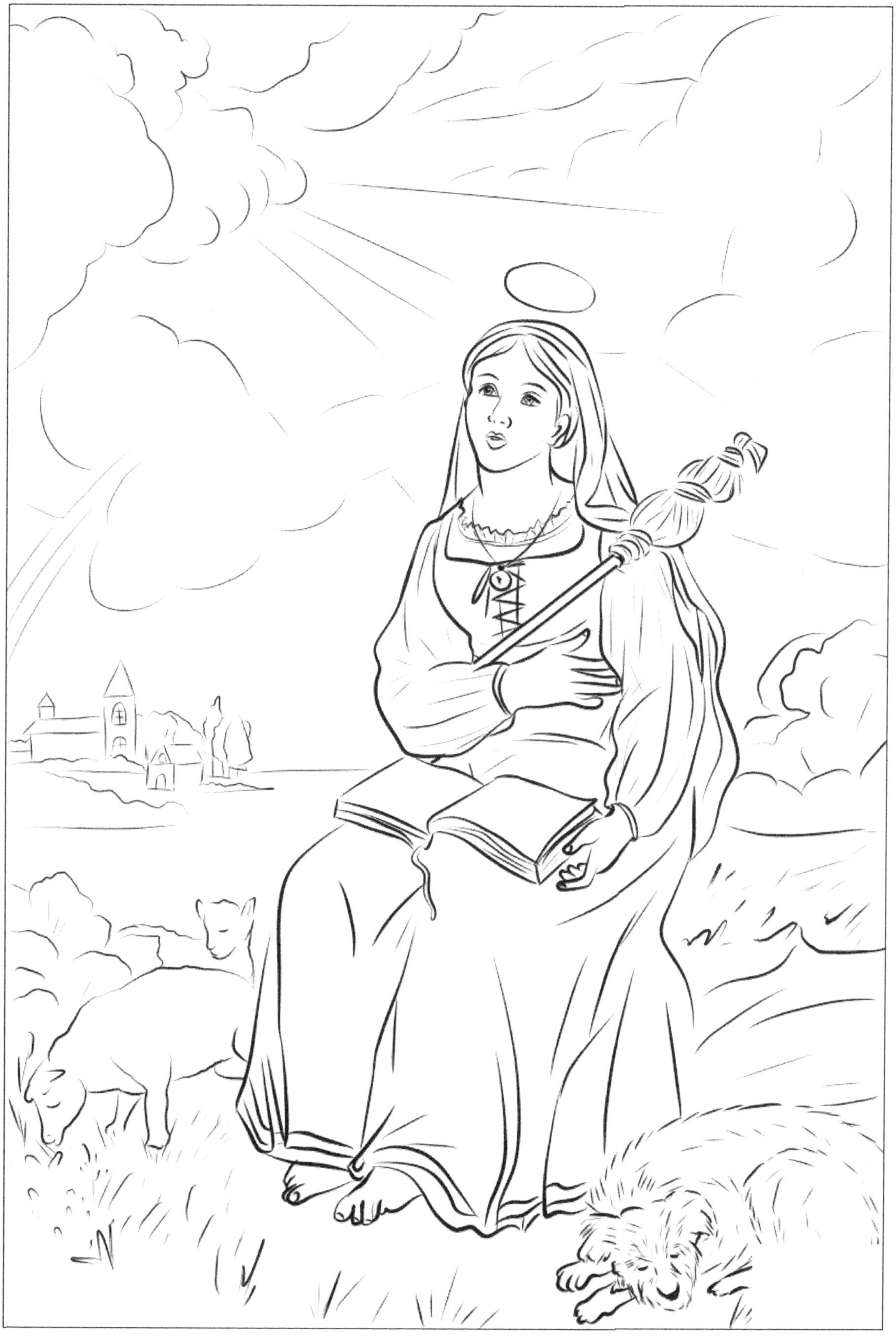

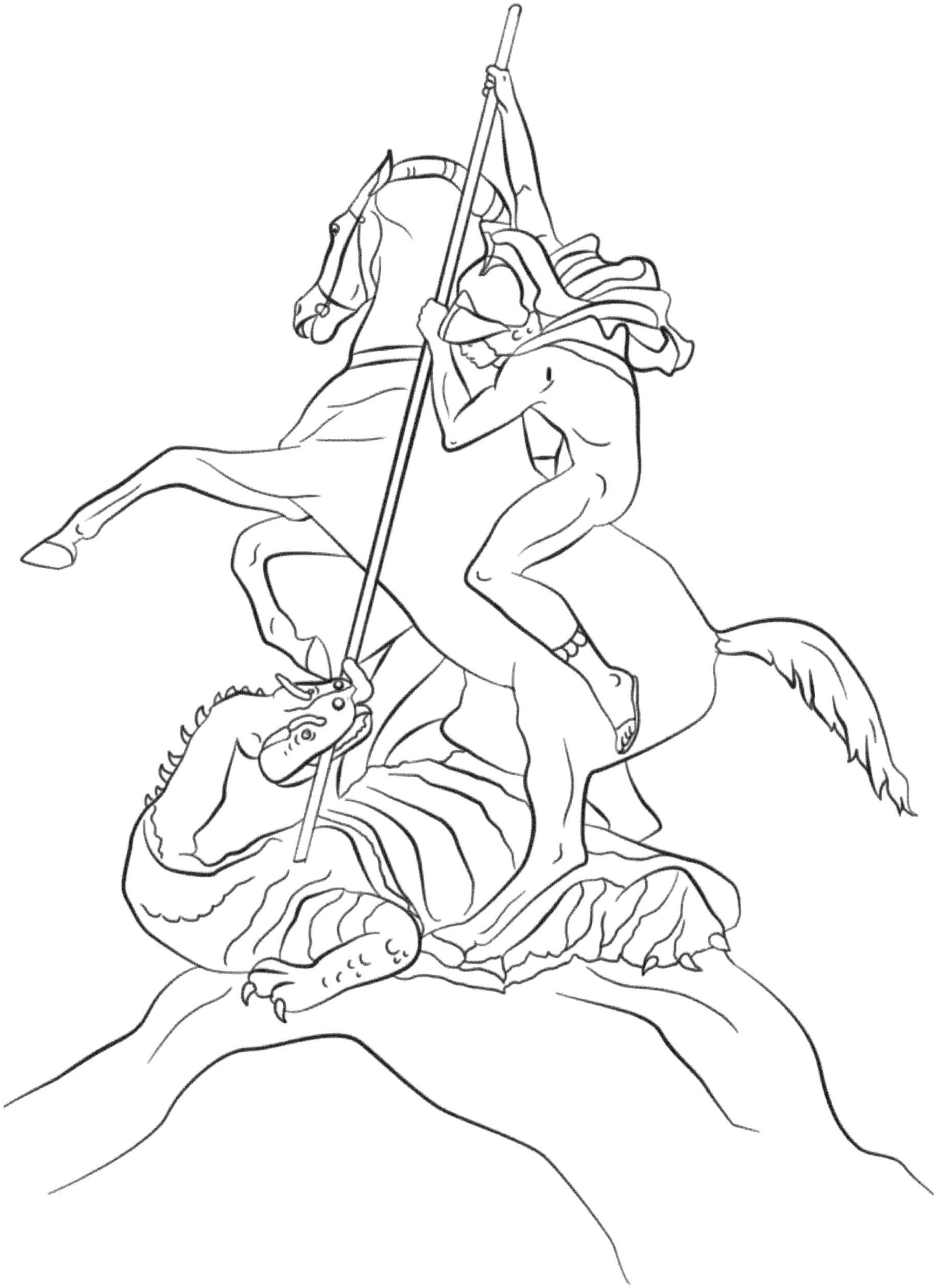

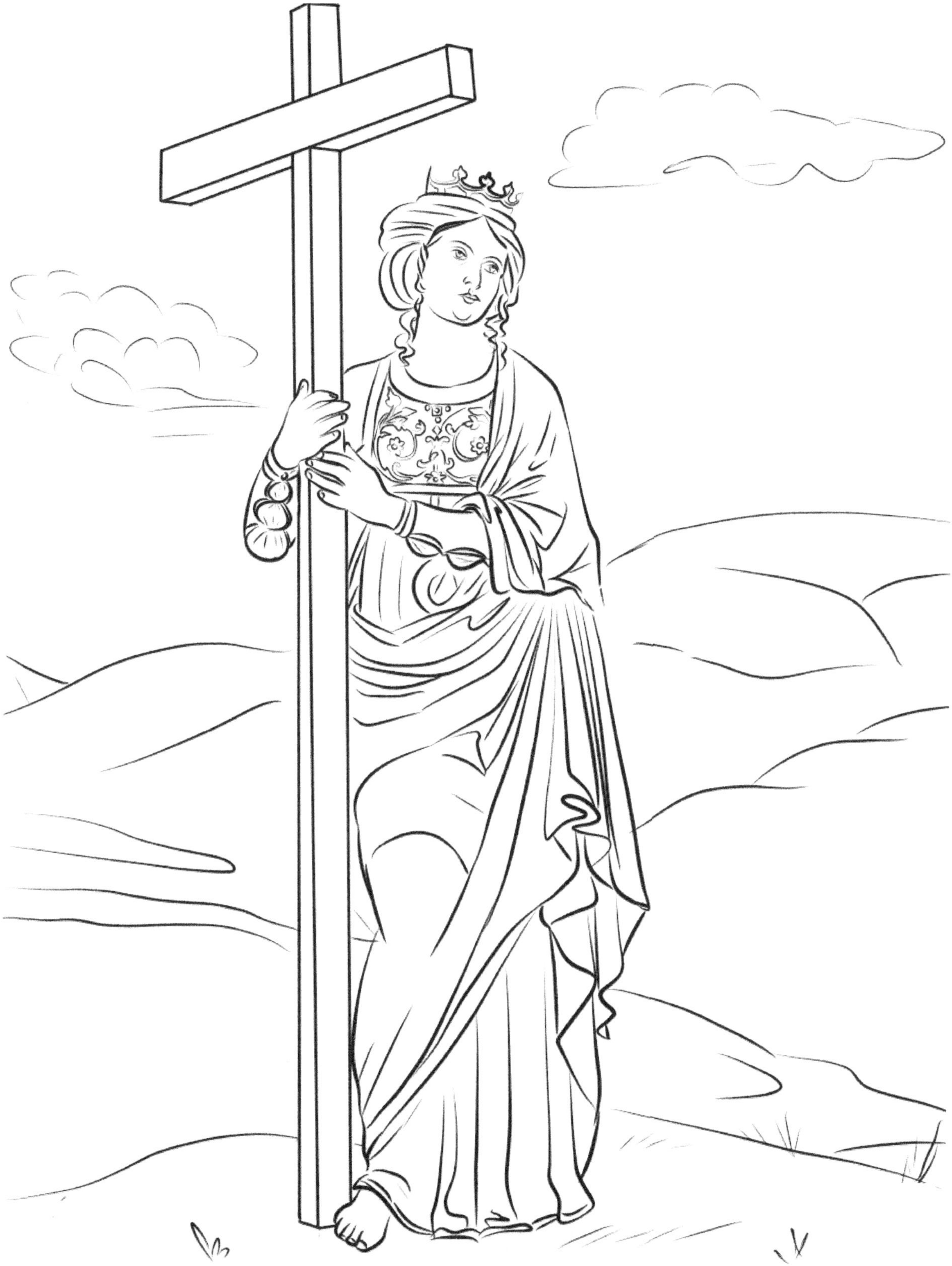

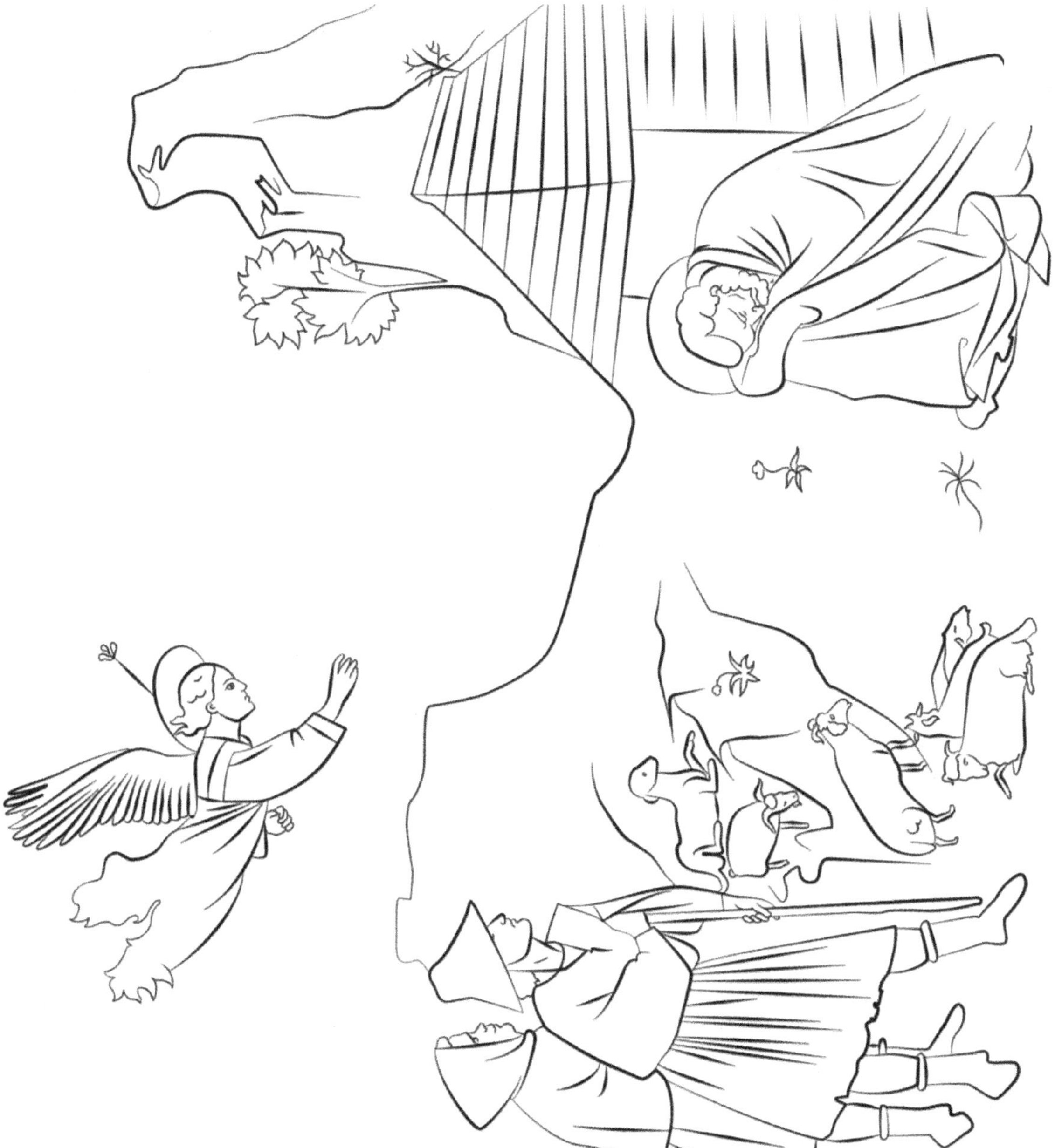

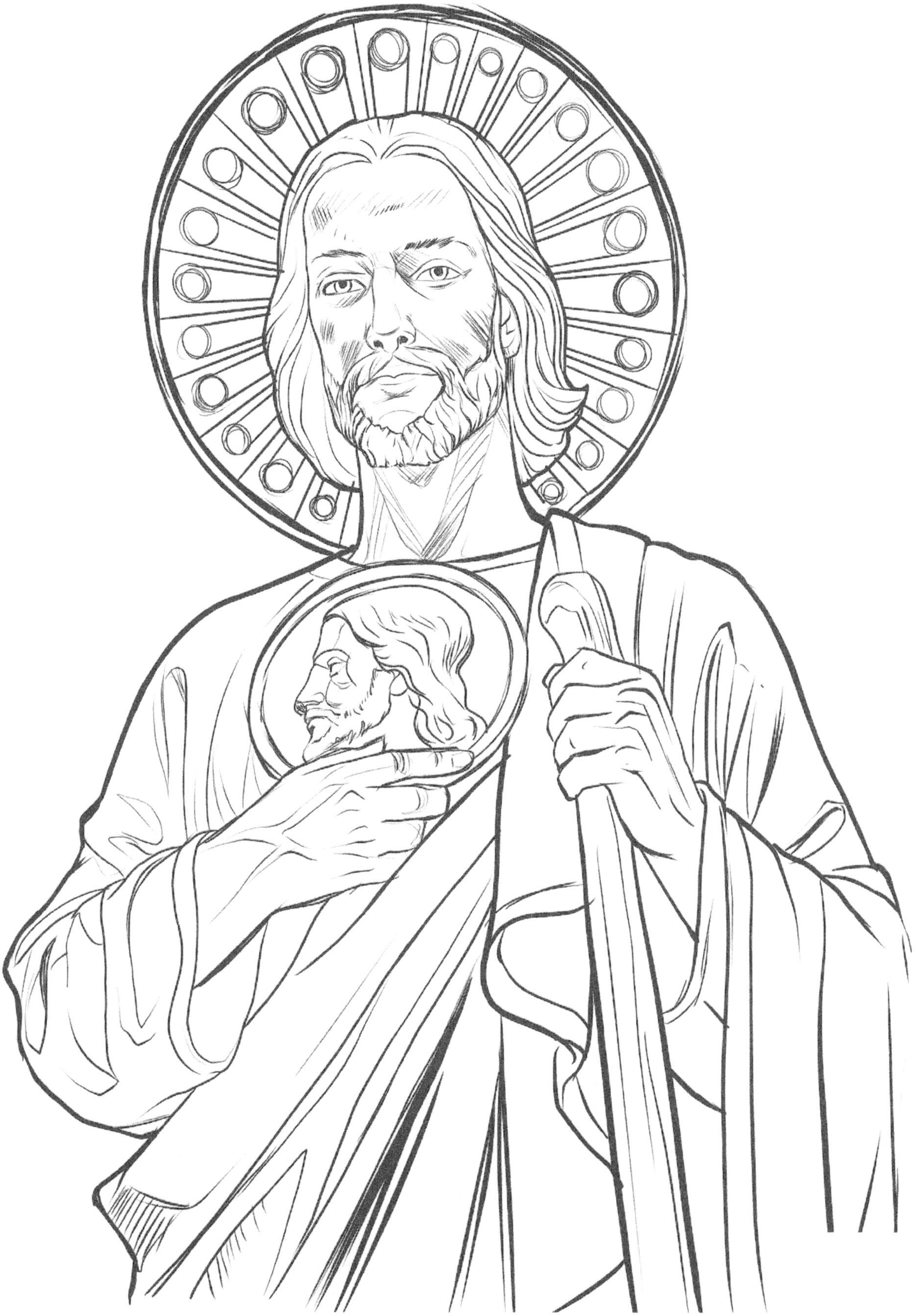

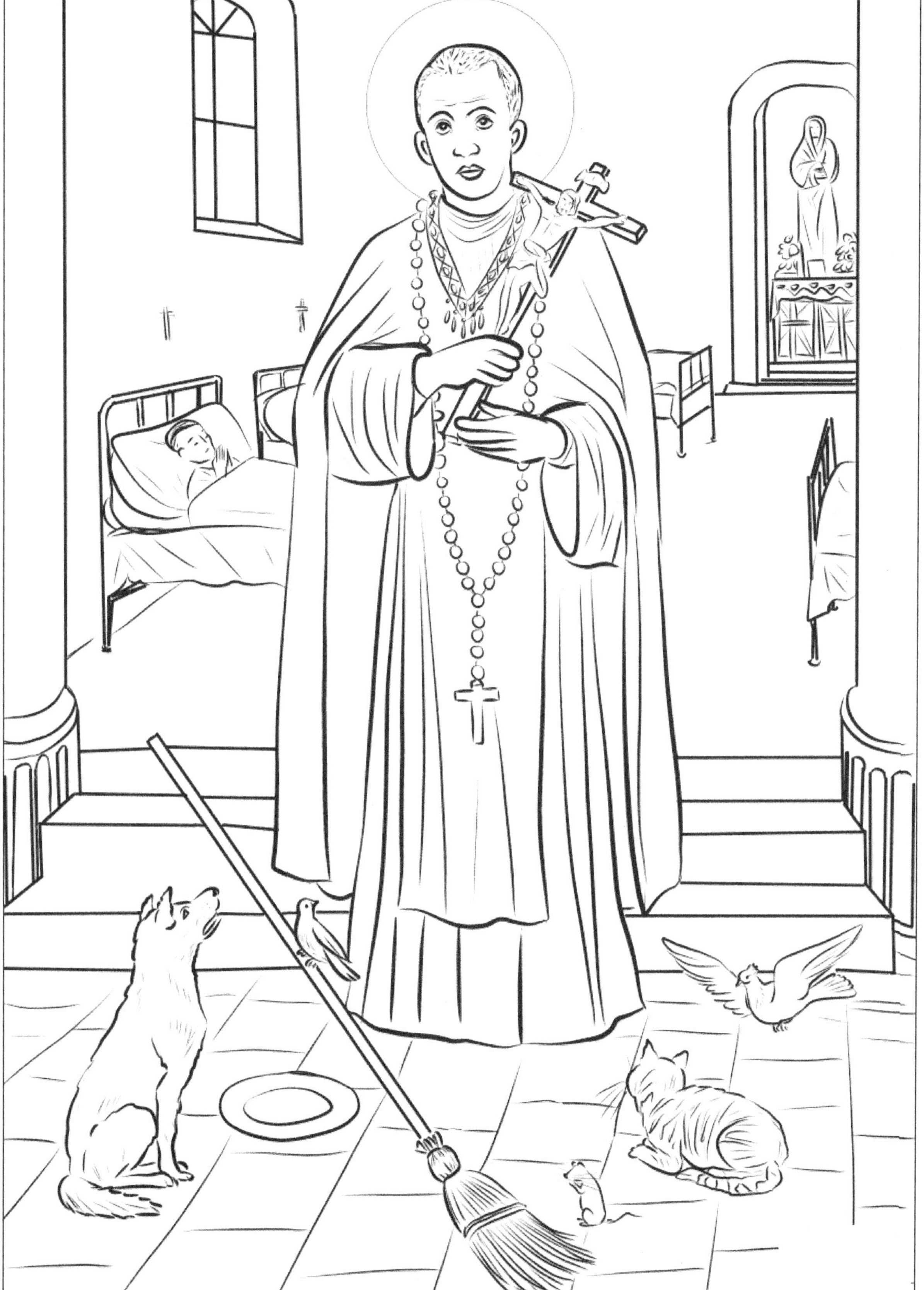

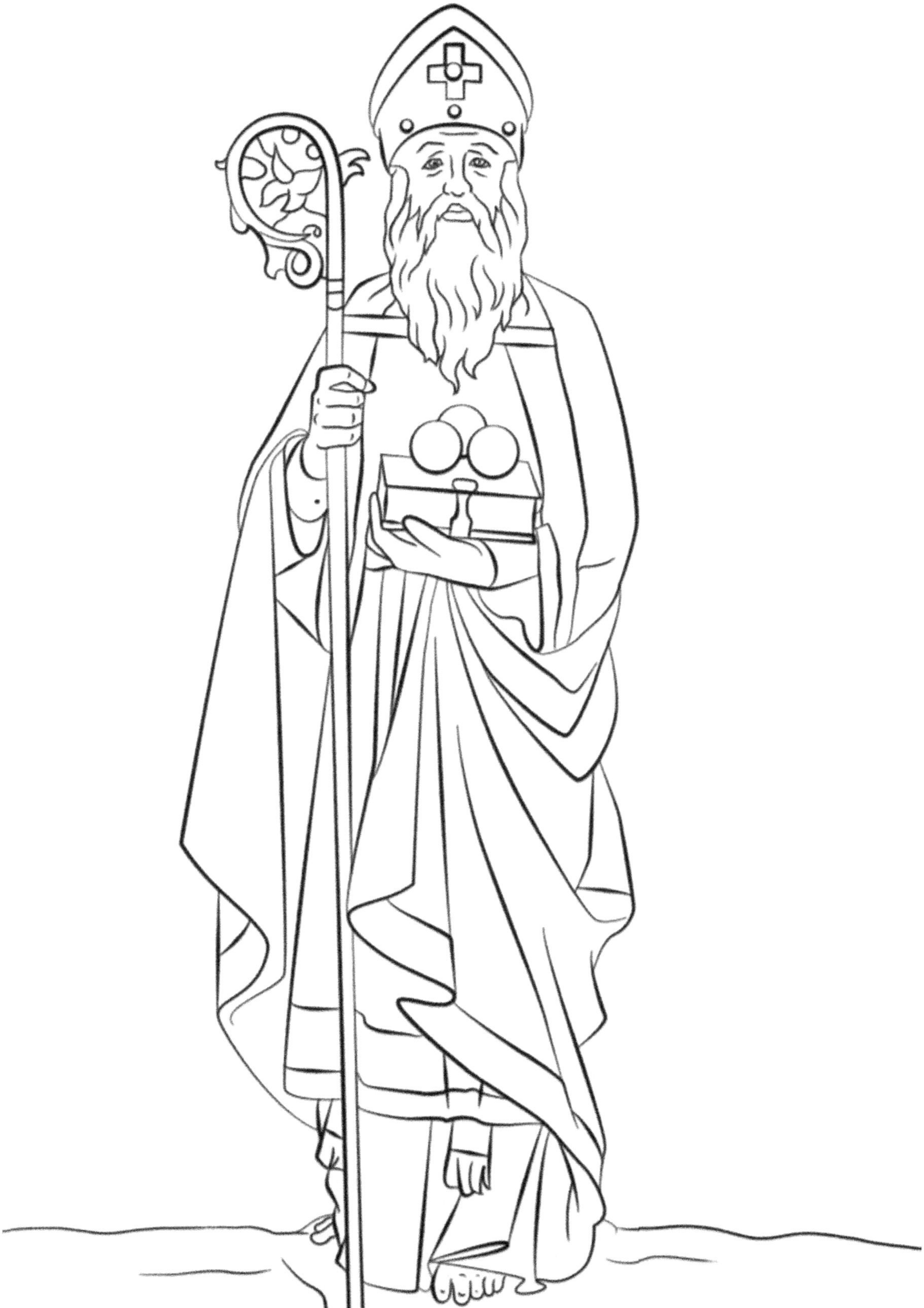

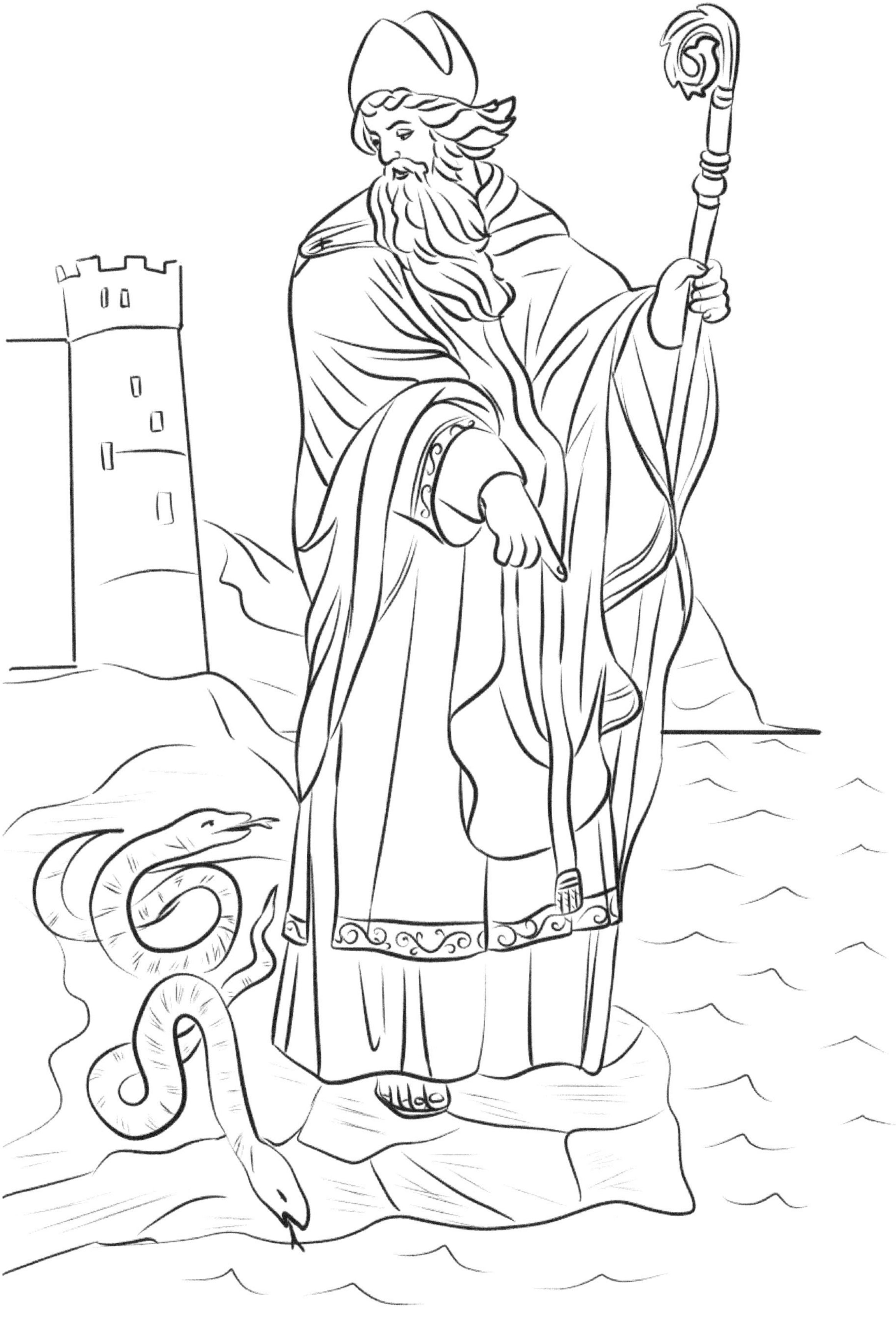

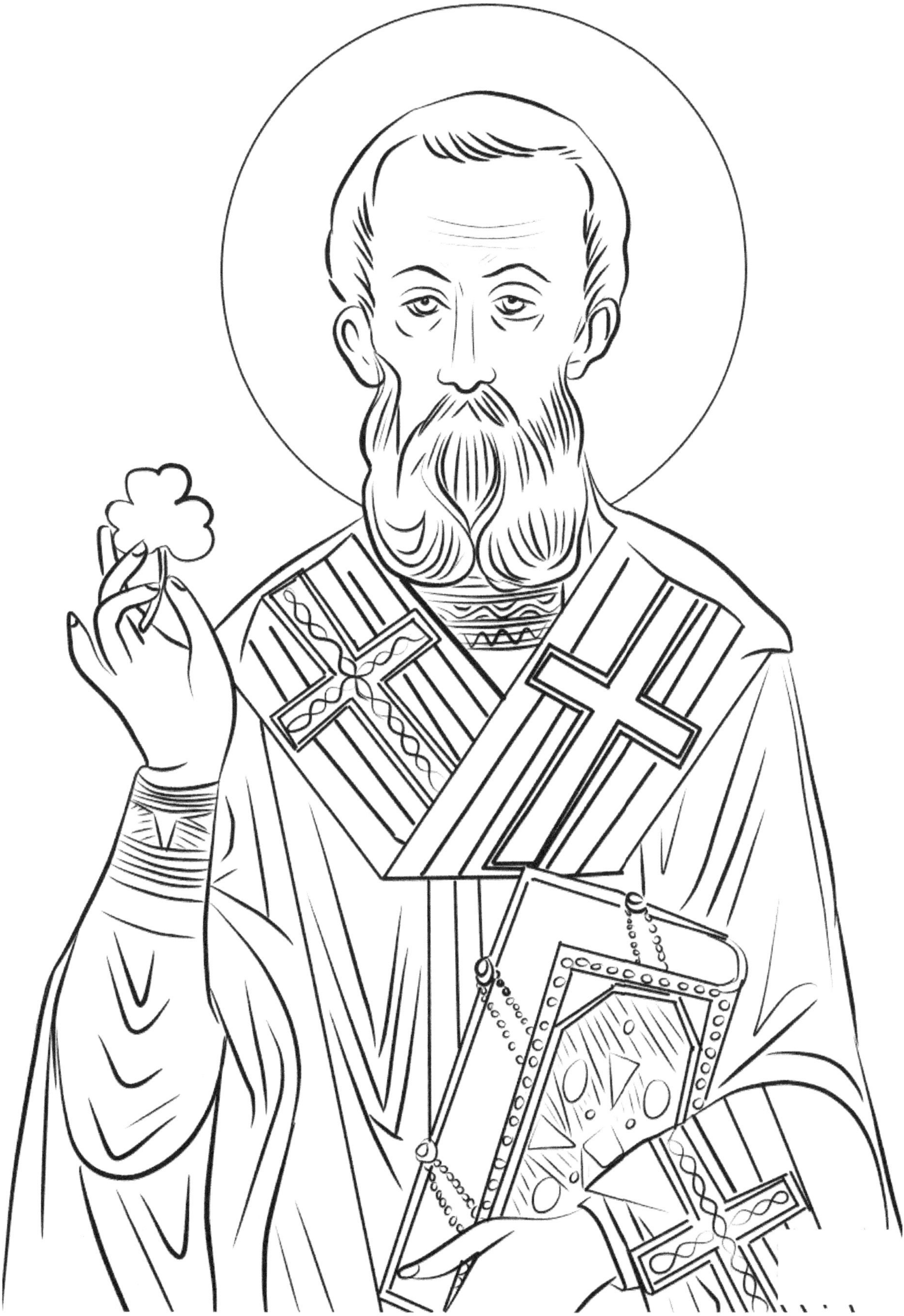

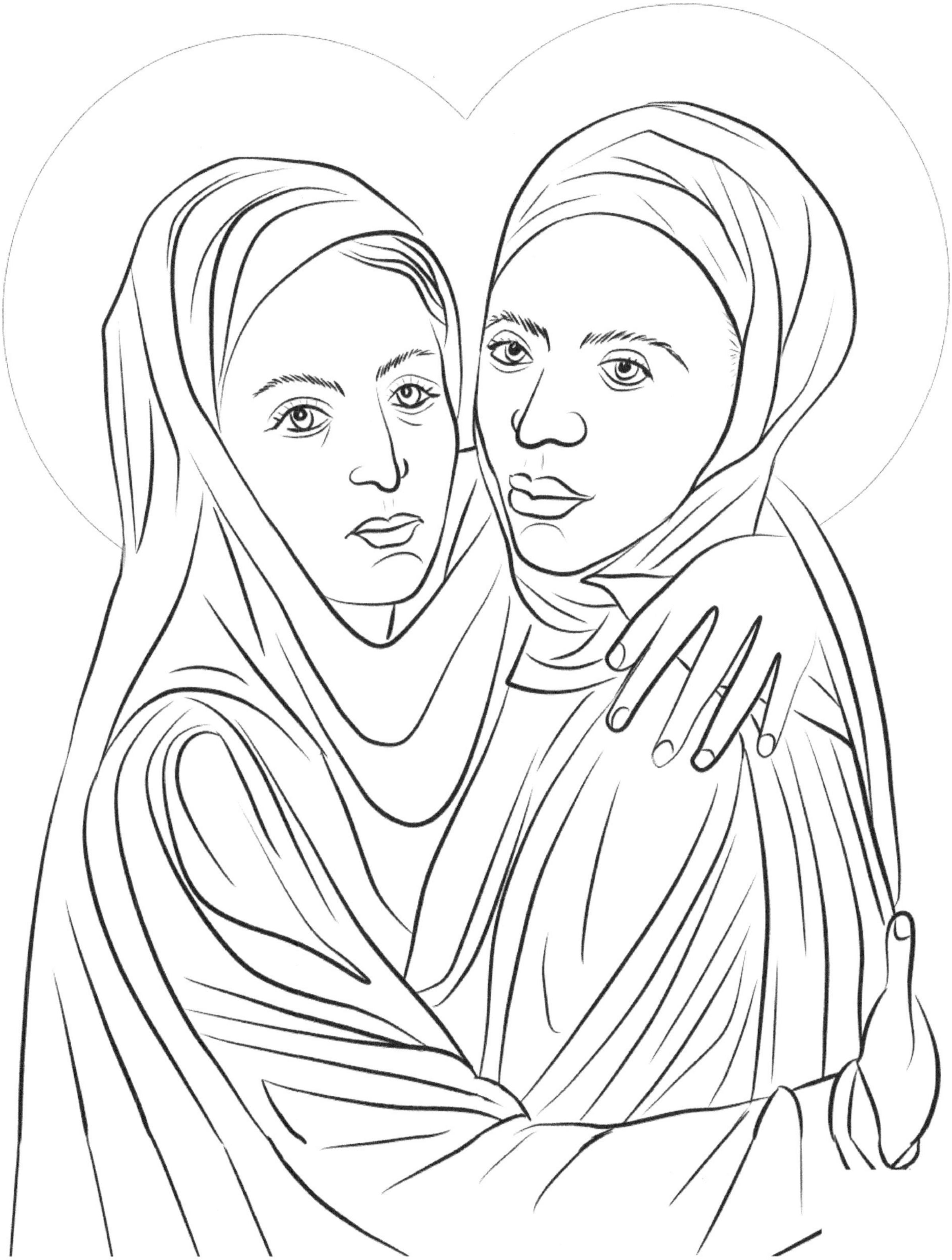

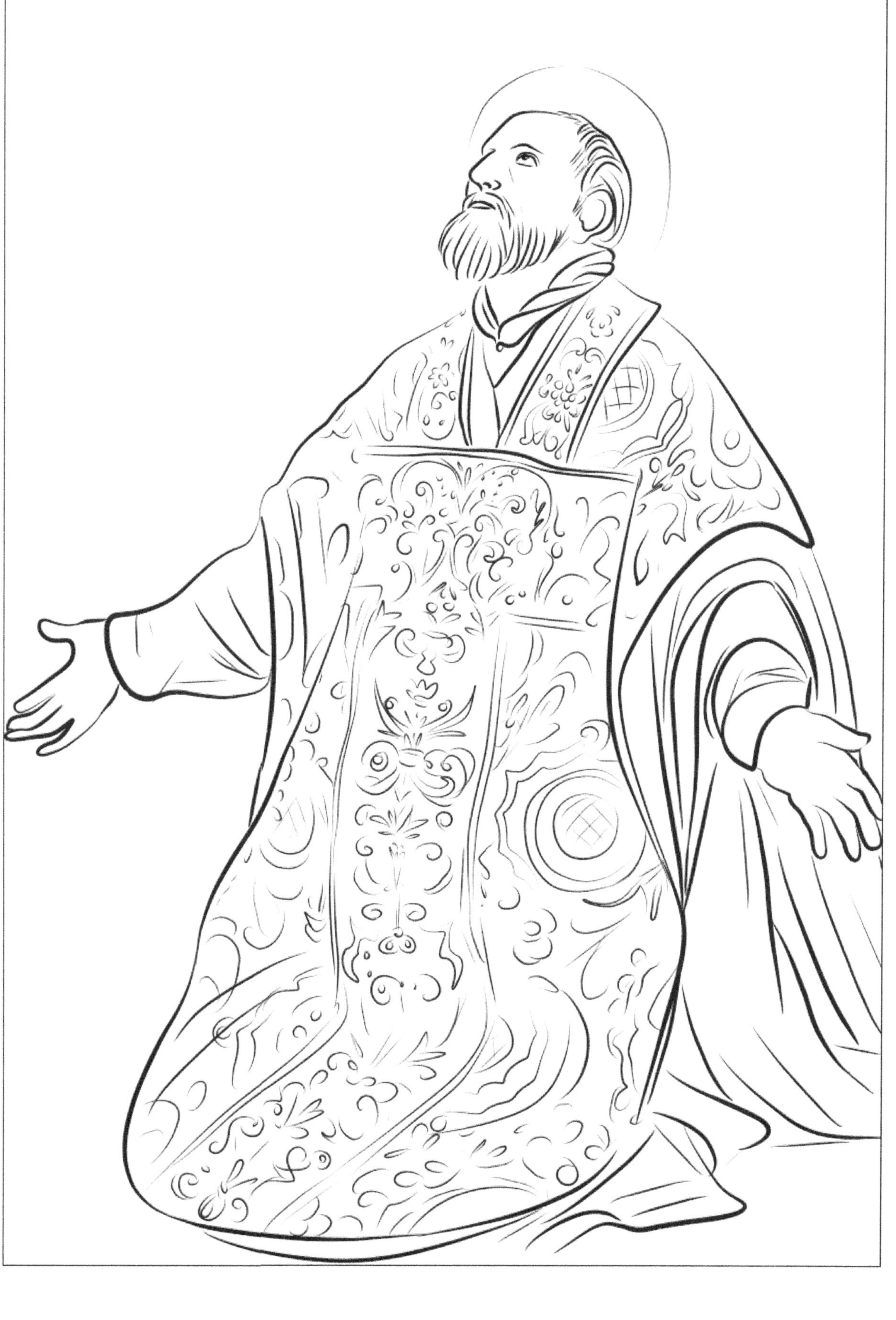

Made in the USA
Middletown, DE
28 September 2021

49229092R00057